Cambridge Elements ≡

Elements in Ethics
edited by
Ben Eggleston
University of Kansas
Dale E. Miller
Old Dominion University, Virginia

CONTRACTUALISM

Jussi Suikkanen
University of Birmingham

CAMBRIDGE
UNIVERSITY PRESS

CAMBRIDGE
UNIVERSITY PRESS

University Printing House, Cambridge CB2 8BS, United Kingdom

One Liberty Plaza, 20th Floor, New York, NY 10006, USA

477 Williamstown Road, Port Melbourne, VIC 3207, Australia

314–321, 3rd Floor, Plot 3, Splendor Forum, Jasola District Centre,
New Delhi – 110025, India

79 Anson Road, #06–04/06, Singapore 079906

Cambridge University Press is part of the University of Cambridge.

It furthers the University's mission by disseminating knowledge in the pursuit of education, learning, and research at the highest international levels of excellence.

www.cambridge.org
Information on this title: www.cambridge.org/9781108712699
DOI: 10.1017/9781108670814

First published 2020

A catalogue record for this publication is available from the British Library.

ISBN 978-1-108-71269-9 Paperback
ISSN 2516-4031 (online)
ISSN 2516-4023 (print)

Contractualism

Elements in Ethics

DOI: 10.1017/9781108670814
First published online: April 2020

Jussi Suikkanen
University of Birmingham

Author for correspondence: Jussi Suikkanen, J.V.Suikkanen@bham.ac.uk

Abstract: This Element begins by describing T. M. Scanlon's contractualism according to which an action is right when it is authorised by the moral principles no one could reasonably reject. This view has been argued to have implausible consequences with regards to how different-sized groups, non-human animals, and cognitively limited human beings should be treated. It has also been accused of being theoretically redundant and unable to vindicate the so-called deontic distinctions. I then distinguish between the general contractualist framework and Scanlon's version of contractualism. I explain how the general framework enables us to formulate many other versions of contractualism, some of which can already be found in the literature. Understanding contractualism in this new way enables us both to understand the structural similarities and differences between different versions of contractualism and to see the different objections to contractualism as internal debates about which version of contractualism is correct.

Keywords: contractualism, ethical theory, moral philosophy, normative ethics, T. M. Scanlon

ISBNs: 9781108712699 (PB), 9781108670814 (OC)
ISSNs: 2516-4031 (online), 2516-4023 (print)

Contents

1 Introduction

This Element has two aims. It first intends to bring its reader up to speed with the recent developments in contractualist ethical theorising. The idea of understanding morality in terms of a contract is old. It was described in Plato's masterpiece the *Republic* about 2,400 years ago (Plato, *Republic*: 358e–359b). Different social contract theories were also popular during the early modern period (1500–1800) when Thomas Hobbes (1651/1996), John Locke (1689/2002), Jean-Jacques Rousseau (1762/1997) and many others developed these theories further.

This Element, however, focusses only on the most recent discussions of contractualism. They tend to begin with a version of contractualism, which T. M. Scanlon introduced in 'Contractualism and Utilitarianism' (1982) and then developed further in *What We Owe to Each Other* (1998). Section 2 outlines Scanlon's theory, which is based on the moral principles no one could reasonably reject. Section 3 then explains the main objections to Scanlon's contractualism. It has been argued that his theory has implausible consequences with respect to how different-sized groups, non-human animals and cognitively limited human beings are to be treated. It has also been claimed that Scanlon's contractualism cannot vindicate the so-called deontic distinctions and that it is merely a redundant theoretical device that is not needed for understanding right and wrong.

Scanlon's contractualism is, of course, not the only contemporary version of contractualism. Thus, in Section 5.2, I outline Derek Parfit's (2011) Kantian contractualism, Nicholas Southwood's (2010) deliberative contractualism and David Gauthier's (1986) contractarianism. I explain both what is common to these contractualist views and how they differ from one another. Thus, by reading Sections 2–3 and 5.2 (as well as Section 5.4, which discusses contractualist responses to the main objections to contractualism), the reader should be able to understand the key issues in the recent debates about contractualism in normative ethics.

This Element, however, also makes an original contribution. It begins from the observation that ethicists have recently come to understand contractualism's main competitor, consequentialism, in a new way. Instead of taking consequentialism to be a distinct view of which actions are right and wrong, many have started to think of it as a flexible framework in which different ethical views can be formulated as versions of consequentialism. The so-called consequentialisers have tried to show that, for every plausible first-order ethical view, there is a version of consequentialism that is co-extensive with it (Dreier, 2011). This so-called consequentialising project promises that the previous debates concerning which ethical theory is true can now be translated into disagreements over which version of consequentialism is correct. Section 4 summarises these recent radical developments.

Section 5 then suggests that we should revise our understanding of contractualism in the same way. It argues that we should draw a distinction between different versions of contractualism (including Scanlon's contractualism) and the general framework of contractualism in which different versions of contractualism can be formulated. This allows us both to explain more precisely how contractualist ethical theories differ from consequentialist theories and to state the differences between different versions of contractualism more accurately.

Section 5.3 furthermore argues that the contractualist framework is just as flexible as the consequentialist one. It turns out that, for every plausible ethical view, there is likewise a version of contractualism that is co-extensive with it. Section 5.4 goes on to explain how this result has radical consequences for our understanding of the traditional objections to contractualism. The previous disagreements over these objections can now be understood as internal questions concerning which version of contractualism is most plausible.

Finally, Section 6 concludes by first summarising the main discussions of this Element. It also considers what consequences these new developments in our understanding of the traditional ethical theories will have for future debates in normative ethics. I suggest that we should no longer argue over which ethical theory is in some general sense true or correct. This is because it is likely that there is a version of every major ethical theory that corresponds to the correct view of which actions are right and wrong. Rather, we should take seriously the idea that, when we try to solve difficult new ethical problems, these theories as general frameworks direct our attention to different kinds of considerations. The consequentialist framework makes us investigate which theories of value are plausible, whereas the contractualist framework guides us to consider what kinds of views of reasons or rationality we should accept. My pragmatic suggestion, then, is that we should accept ethical theories on the basis of how helpful the ways of thinking about new ethical problems they provide are. I also recommend accepting a form of pluralism. In advance, we have no reason to think that one framework of ethical theorising will be the most fruitful one in every context. Rather, different ethical views may well enable us to investigate different problem cases in more illuminating ways.

2 Scanlon's Contractualism

This section begins by reconstructing Scanlon's contractualism on the basis of how it was presented in *What We Owe to Each Other*.[1] Scanlon's starting point is that any plausible ethical theory ought to answer two questions at the same time (147–9). Such a theory should first be able to provide a plausible view of which actions are right and wrong. After all, any plausible ethical theory should entail, for example, that we ought to keep our promises. At the same time, a plausible ethical theory should also be able to explain *why* we ought to do what is right and avoid acting wrongly. Scanlon does not understand this second question as a psychological question that is about which mental states move us to do the right thing but rather as a question concerning normative reasons (148). What are the '(almost?) always' overriding reasons we have for acting morally?

Providing a satisfactory answer to this second question is difficult due to 'Prichard's dilemma' (149–53; Prichard, 1912). We cannot merely claim that we should do right actions because they are right. This answer would merely take the reason-providing force of morality for granted. We cannot, however, offer merely non-moral reasons for why we ought to do the right thing either. Purely self-interested reasons based, for example, on the costs of being ostracised by others would simply not be the right kinds of reasons. They would not be the kinds of reasons we intuitively take ourselves to have for acting morally. The challenge is thus to provide an account of our reasons for doing the right thing that is at the same time both informative and recognisably moral in nature.

Scanlon's contractualism thus attempts to describe the nature of rightness and wrongness in a way that both (1) makes sense of which actions are right and wrong and (2) explains why we ought to do right actions understood in that way.[2] He believes that we should begin from what we can justify to others on

---

[1] All unattributed references are to Scanlon (1998). In addition to contractualism, Scanlon's book addresses a number of other topics including the nature of value (of which he gives a buck-passing account), the nature of well-being and the role of teleology in practical reasoning. It is true that these views also to a large extent underwrite Scanlon's own version of contractualism, and so Scanlon's discussions of these topics are essential reading for anyone interested in Scanlon's contractualism.

[2] In *What We Owe to Each Other*, Scanlon explicitly presented his view as a metaethical or metaphysical theory of the nature of the properties of rightness and wrongness (12) that constitutes the subject matter of our judgements of right and wrong (2). He then considers being able to make sense of which actions are right and wrong and being able to explain the reasons for acting rightly to be the standard by which to evaluate the previous kind of metaphysical/metaethical theories of the nature of right and wrong. Later on, he acknowledged that he 'should have avoided describing contractualism as an account of the property of moral wrongness' in the previous way (Scanlon, 2004: 137). His more recent proposal is to understand contractualism as a view of which standards we should use to evaluate our actions and what reasons support these

grounds they could not reasonably reject (153–5).[3] He then argues that focussing on this type of idealised justification will enable us to explain both which actions are right and what reasons we have for doing those actions. Next, in Section 2.1, I focus on how Scanlon derives an account of right and wrong from the previous type of justification. Section 2.2 then outlines how that account can be used to answer the question of why we should be moral.

2.1 Which Actions Are Right?

How could we then get from justification to an account of which actions are right and wrong? Let us use a simplistic version of contractualism as a starting point. When our actions affect others, they often question what we have done to them. In such cases, it clearly helps if you can explain *why* you did what you did in a way that the other person accepts. If others accept your reasons, they will no longer disapprove of what you did, which leads to pleasant harmony (154).

As a consequence, you might think that we could explain what is right and wrong by relying on which justifications others actually accept. This starting point would allow us to explain what reasons we have for doing the right thing – right actions will help us to avoid conflicts and they also lead to harmonious social interaction. Starting from actual justification would furthermore lead to a view of which actions are right and wrong. Right actions would be precisely the ones we can justify to others on grounds they accept.

This proposal admittedly has advantages. Firstly, whether an action is right becomes a tractable empirical question concerning which justifications others accept on the basis of what they ultimately care about. Secondly, as we have just seen, the view offers at least some kind of an explanation of why we ought to do the actions that are right in the relevant sense. The reason for doing those actions is that acting in those ways makes our interactions with other people run more smoothly, which often is in our selfish interests.

According to Scanlon, the previous proposal has one fundamental flaw (155). The problem is that it leads to an implausible account of which actions are right and wrong. Some individuals, as a matter of fact, do not think that their own interests are as important as the interests of others. These individuals are so modest that they are often happy to receive less than others, and sometimes they

---

standards (ibid.). This fits with the description of his project given in Sections 2.1 and 2.2 in this Element.

[3] The idea of justifiability to others thus plays a crucial role in Scanlon's own version of contractualism. In Section 5.1, I have suggested that, despite this, this notion should not be thought to be what makes a theory a version of contractualism. This is because there are versions of consequentialism that equally rely on the idea (see Hooker, 2000: 99–102) and versions of contractualism that do not (Southwood, 2010).

do not even object to being treated badly. The previous simple view would entail that it would be morally right to give these modest, self-sacrificing individuals less than others and sometimes it would not even be wrong to mistreat these individuals as long as they accept such mistreatment. For this simple reason, the previous simple view fails as a view of which actions are right.

Right and wrong cannot, therefore, be a matter of which actions can be justified to others on grounds they actually accept. We can then think of Scanlon's own theory as an attempt to formulate a more sophisticated view that could avoid the problems of the previous simple view. Scanlon believes that we can still make sense of right and wrong in terms of what can be justified to others. However, instead of actual justification, according to him, we will have to focus on which actions we can justify to others on grounds *they could not reasonably reject*. Even if the self-sacrificing individuals accepted our attempts to justify the ways in which we mistreat them, they still *could* reasonably reject those justifications. This is why the reformulated view does not entail that treating self-sacrificing individuals badly is right.

According to Scanlon's contractualism, therefore, actions are right insofar as they are authorised by the set of moral principles no one could reasonably reject (and wrong insofar as they are forbidden by those principles) (4–5, 153). We, of course, want to know next what would make a set of moral principles one that could not be reasonably rejected. This is easiest to explain with a simple case (195).[4] Imagine that you and I are considering whether acting in a certain way (φing) would be wrong in the circumstances (C) we are in. According to Scanlon, we then first need to compare different principles that could be adopted to govern φing in different C-like circumstances.

The relevant principles we could adopt should not be understood merely as simple, absolute and exceptionless principles of the form 'Always φ!' or 'Never φ'. Rather, it is better to understand them as complex elements that could be added to our overall moral sensitivities, where these elements determine in part whether φing would be seen as the thing to do in different situations. These elements of our moral sensitivities determine when the relevant rule applies, what exceptions it allows and what strength it has in different cases of conflict (197–202; see also Hooker, 2000: 90–1).

Let us then consider two alternative principles – one that would authorise us to φ (hereafter 'the permitting rule') and one that would forbid φing ('the forbidding rule'). According to Scanlon, the next step is to examine what consequences the general adoption of these principles would have for different

---

[4] Here, for the sake of simplicity and for illustrative purposes, I focus on comparing individual principles rather than whole sets of principles (as properly speaking I should).

individuals (195, 202–6). After all, the general adoption of the permitting rule and the general adoption of the forbidding rule would mean that people would act in different ways. As a result, which principle we adopted would eventually make a difference to what kinds of lives we, as individuals, would come to live.

For example, imagine that φing is something that is mildly amusing to do to others, trivially harmful for the victims in individual cases and seriously harmful for people who are repeatedly treated in that way. In this case, it is easy to see that people come to live very different kinds of lives depending on whether the permitting rule or the forbidding rule is adopted. In the scenario in which the permitting rule is adopted, some people benefit a little because they are able to φ, whereas others suffer the trivial harms that together constitute a serious burden to them over time. In contrast, when the forbidding rule is adopted both the trivial benefits and the resulting serious harms go away.

Scanlon calls the lives which individuals come to live under the alternative principles their 'standpoints' (202). Furthermore, we can call 'burdens' the features of these standpoints that make them less choice-worthy as lives (195). These burdensome features of the lives of different individuals then provide those individuals with reasons to make objections to the principles that are causally responsible for the burdens in question. For instance, in the previous example, the individuals who repeatedly suffer a minor loss because others φ can use the burden of having to suffer all those losses as an objection to the adoption of the permitting rule.

Scanlon's theory of reasonable rejectability still needs two further elements. Firstly, we need an account of which features of the lives of different individuals ground legitimate objections to different moral principles (213–18). Here, Scanlon seems to rule out two kinds of considerations and explicitly include at least two others. Firstly, on the pain of vicious circularity and redundancy (see Section 3.4.1), the fact that others would wrong you by φing cannot be a feature of your standpoint that enables you to object to the permitting rule. After all, when you give an account of what is right and wrong, your account cannot rely on rightness and wrongness of different actions. We can call this the 'deontic restriction' on the reasons to reject principles (216; see also Parfit, 2003: 370). Secondly, your reasons for making objections to a given moral principle must be features of your own life. Your reason to object to a principle cannot be based on the combined, aggregate burden that both you and some other people are burdened in a certain way by the adoption of that principle.[5] Call this the

---

[5] This condition does not preclude counting the empathic pain I would feel because of someone else's suffering as a burden which can ground an objection to a moral principle. However, usually such an objection is considered to be weaker than the one based on the original suffering that causes me to feel the empathic pain in the first place.

'individualist restriction' on the reasons to reject principles (229; see also Ridge, 2001).

What would then count as a legitimate reason? Firstly, Scanlon accepts that, if a principle lowers your level of well-being, you can make an objection to that principle on that basis (216). However, he denies that well-being would be the only ground for an objection. He also rejects the idea that well-being would provide a master currency that could be used to weigh different objections. Scanlon instead claims that we should consider more concrete qualities of individual lives as the relevant burdens that count as 'generic' reasons to make objections to different principles. These more concrete personal considerations include, for example, bodily harms, not being able to rely on the assurances of others and not having control over what happens to one's own body (204). These considerations count as generic reasons because their status as a reason does not depend on particular aims or preferences of individuals.

Scanlon also accepts that, when we compare moral principles, individuals can also make objections on the basis of other moral rules that are not at issue in the comparison in question (214). When we evaluate one principle, say, governing our obligation to help those in need, we need to take into account how the adoption of that principle would affect what people are entitled to on the basis of other moral principles. To assess one principle, we thus need to hold at least some other principles fixed. Of course, those other principles can also be evaluated in the contractualist comparisons of different principles but, when we do so, we again need to hold at least some other principles fixed.

We then have a sense of what kinds of objections individuals can make to different principles. Which principles cannot then be reasonably rejected? Here, we must consider the strongest personal objections which individuals can make to the different alternatives. We must first identify the individuals who would be personally burdened the most by the general adoption of every principle that could potentially govern a certain kind of situation. This is because these individuals could make the strongest objections to those principles. We then compare pairwise the strength of the personal reasons which these individuals have for rejecting the relevant principles (195). The individuals who have the stronger reasons to make objections in these comparisons can reasonably reject the principles that are making their lives burdensome. In contrast, the one person whose objection is grounded on the weakest personal reason cannot do so, because some individuals would always have stronger personal objections to all other moral principles that could potentially govern the relevant type of situations (229).

To see how this works, recall that in the earlier example the general adoption of the permitting principle would provide minor benefits to some even if it would also make the lives of many people more burdensome over time. In this case, those individuals could make a serious objection to the permitting principle, whereas no one could make an equally strong objection to the forbidding principle (no one would lose more than a minor benefit if that principle were adopted). In Scanlon's view, the forbidding principle could thus not be reasonably rejected because there would be stronger personal objections to the alternative. Moral principles that no one could reasonably reject are therefore more generally such that there are stronger personal reasons to reject all the principles that could replace them.

If there are many different principles that could govern certain kinds of situations to which the most serious personal objections are equally the least serious, we need to consider to which of these principles the fewest individuals could make those objections (230–4). If there still are many principles to which equally many individuals could make the most serious personal objection, we need to compare the second most serious objections in the same way. If these objections and their number are also tied, we keep moving to the less serious objections until we find a unique principle that could not be reasonably rejected because all other principles would produce more serious unnecessary burdens to some individuals.

Scanlon's claim, then, is that understanding right and wrong in terms of the previous non-rejectable principles gives us an extensionally adequate account of right and wrong. The view would fit our moral intuitions as the following illustrations are supposed to show.

Firstly, the previous theory promises to make sense of the wrongness of promise-breaking (295–327). When you make a promise, you knowingly create expectations in the other person to whom you make the promise. Breaking the promise will mean that those expectations will not be met. Consider, then, two potential principles that could govern promise-breaking: a forbidding rule and a permitting one. If we all adopted the latter rule and thus believed that there is nothing wrong with breaking a promise, many more promises would not be kept. This would burden many individuals because their expectations, which the relevant promises had created, would not be met. In this scenario, we would also lose the ability to rely on the assurances of others. We would just not believe them when they would try to make a promise. This presumably would make our lives more difficult in a number of ways.

In contrast, there would not be equally strong objections to the forbidding rule. It is difficult to see how the burden of having to keep a promise could be claimed to be unreasonable. This is because there is always an easy way to avoid that burden – all you need to do is not to make the promise in the first place. We must, of course, recognise that in some situations it is permissible to break a promise. For example, you are not required to keep your promise to meet your friend at a café if keeping that promise would require not saving the easily saveable drowning child on your way. One promise of contractualism is that it will help us to understand this type of exception to the promise-keeping principle. After all, as the previous example shows, the most stringent principles could be reasonably rejected because they would cause certain serious personal burdens to some individuals, which no one would need to experience under the less stringent principles that contain some exceptions to the general requirement.

Scanlon also argues that his contractualism fits our intuitions about the so-called *anti-utilitarian protections*, according to which morality does not allow us to sacrifice individuals for the sake of the general good. Consider Scanlon's own example in which millions of people are enjoying watching the World Cup final live on television (235). Unfortunately, a piece of equipment falls on Jones in the transmitter room. As a result, Jones is receiving extremely painful electric shocks. The only way to help him is to cut off the transmission for 15 minutes. This would mean denying millions of people the pleasure of watching the final.

Many people agree that the right thing to do is to save Jones. Scanlon's contractualism promises to tell us just why we ought to do so. We must again begin by comparing two principles that could govern the situation. The strongest objection any person could make to the principle that requires saving Jones is that this principle would require them to give up the trivial benefit of being able to follow the match. Yet Jones clearly has a much stronger objection to the principle that would forbid saving him based on the painful electric shocks. Given that the 'Save Jones!' principle would not cause equally serious burdens to anyone, that principle could not be reasonably rejected. Contractualism, due to the individualist restriction, thus does not allow us to sacrifice individuals like Jones for the sake of the general good.[6]

These are, of course, just two cases in which Scanlon's contractualism seems to have appealing consequences. Scanlon's hope, however, is that, whatever intuitively wrong kind of an action we take, we can always identify some serious personal burdens on the basis of which some individuals could reasonably reject the principles that would permit that kind of action. If we are always able to identify the previous kind of burden, then considering which principles could not be reasonably rejected seems to offer us a compelling account of right and wrong.

---

[6] In Scanlon's view, objections are always compared one-to-one. This entails that the only way that the fact that an option would burden many people could be taken into account would be if one person could include the other people's burdens into their objection. The individualist restriction rules this out.

2.2 Why Be Moral?

As discussed, Scanlon believes that a plausible ethical theory should be able to explain why we ought to do the right thing when we, at the same time, use that same theory to understand which actions are right.[7] Let us return to the simplistic version of contractualism introduced in Section 2.1. According to it, which actions are right is a function of which justifications others are actually willing to accept. Even if this view fails as an account of which actions are right, it admittedly provides a compelling explanation of why we ought to do right actions where rightness is understood in terms of actual justifiability. Such actions tend to lead to harmony, co-operation and fewer conflicts. Insofar as we then have reasons to live in such a pleasant way with others, we have reasons to do actions that we can justify to others on grounds they accept.

This account of why we ought to be moral is not available for Scanlon, because, in his view, what we can justify to others on grounds they actually accept is not relevant at all. Instead, we are now considering actions that are authorised by the principles no one could reasonably reject. However, even if an action were authorised by those principles, the person affected by the action might not actually accept the justification you offer to them on grounds they could not reasonably reject (and so they would be acting unreasonably, as we often do). This is why following the principles no one could reasonably reject need not lead to actual harmony. The ability to live in harmony with others cannot therefore be our only reason to do the actions that are authorised by the non-rejectable principles.

What, then, are the reasons to follow those principles? Here, three types of reasons are relevant. Firstly, there are almost always concrete first-order reasons not to do actions that are forbidden by the non-rejectable principles (156; see also Stratton-Lake, 2003: 74; Wallace, 2002: 455). The principles that would allow doing those actions could always be reasonably rejected because of some concrete burdens that some individuals would have to bear as a consequence of those principles. Principles that authorised physical attacks would, for example, make some people's lives more burdensome because they would have to suffer the consequences of the attacks which these principles would permit. This suggests that there are always concrete, ordinary first-order reasons not to do

---

[7] So, for example, Scanlon recognises that utilitarianism can, in many cases, provide a plausible account of which actions are wrong. For example, utilitarianism correctly entails that we should help people who live in extreme poverty (152). However, Scanlon objects that this is not enough to make utilitarianism a plausible account of what it is for actions to be right and wrong, because utilitarianism fails as an account of the reason-giving force of the idea of moral wrongness (152–3); that is, a plausible account of right and wrong also has to be able to provide a compelling account of just why we ought to avoid acting wrongly.

actions that are forbidden by the non-rejectable principles. These actions tend to affect other individuals in some negative ways – exactly in the same ways that ground the relevant reasonable rejections of the principles that would allow these actions.

Secondly, Scanlon argues that there are also other, more general and abstract higher-order reasons to not do the actions that are forbidden by the non-rejectable principles (162). It is easiest to approach these reasons from Philippa Foot's notion of *second-order evil* (Foot, 1994: 210–11). Foot's idea is that not only do we suffer first-order evil when someone harms us but we can also suffer second-order evil on the basis of being aware that our sound objections to being mistreated are being discarded for no good reason.[8] There is something fundamentally demeaning about not being recognised as someone whose objections need to be taken into account.

The reasons Scanlon claims there are for following the non-rejectable principles are grounded on second-order evil. The claim is that, by following these principles, we can tell others that we *are* taking into account their potential objections to our actions and that we are treating those objections exactly as seriously as everyone else's. Following these principles thus enables us to recognise others as a source of moral reasons – as rational agents whose standpoints, objections and evaluations of objections need to be taken seriously. Scanlon thus argues that, by following the non-rejectable principles, we can form highly valuable moral relationships of 'mutual recognition' (162).[9] Insofar as we then have good reasons to be in those type of relationships with others, we have reasons to follow the non-rejectable principles.

Some people have objected that this account of our reasons to follow the non-rejectable principles is too abstract to explain why we really ought to do the right thing, sometimes even at a considerable cost to ourselves (see Wallace 2002: 454).[10] I believe that there are two ways of trying to address this concern.

---

[8] This idea explains one important appeal of the contractualist ethical theories. In addition to being able to explain which actions are wrong and why we ought not to do those actions, contractualist views of this type can also provide a compelling account of what it is to wrong another agent. Wronging in this view consists of overlooking the other agent's reasonable objections to your actions. See Wallace (2019) for an important development of this idea.

[9] Scanlon himself explored the nature of this relationship relatively little in *What We Owe to Each Other* (160–8). For a more detailed discussion, see Scanlon (2008), especially chap. 4.

[10] It is true that this concern is quite abstract. One way to make it more concrete is to think of cases where we have to choose between doing the right thing and helping our friends or children. In these cases, we know enough about the concrete relationships of friendship and parenthood to get a sense of what reasons there are for helping our friends and children in immoral ways. The problem is that, in Scanlon's view, there is something about the general moral relationship of mutual recognition that is so important that it makes acting morally more important in these cases. Yet it is not clear what that quality of the abstract relationship of mutual recognition is. Scanlon's own way of addressing this issue relies on the idea that all other important

Both of these strategies try to point to a third kind of reason we have for following the principles no one can reasonably reject.

Philip Pettit has explained nicely in more concrete terms just why we value the relationship of mutual recognition (that is, the ability to justify our actions to others on grounds they could not reasonably reject) so highly. As he puts it, it does seem right that 'we shrink from the gaze of another when we realise that it is impossible for us to justify our behaviour to someone else' (Pettit, 2000: 231). Or, in other terms, 'we squirm at any failure to do so' (ibid.), whereas, if we can justify our actions to others on non-rejectable grounds, we can stand by our actions. We can happily look other people in the eyes, which many of us would take to be a considerable concrete good. These intuitions suggest that, at least in some implicit form, we do value the kind of relationship Scanlon is describing.

James Lenman (2006: 16–20) has also explained in an illuminating way what other, more concrete instrumental reasons we can have for following the non-rejectable principles. Lenman emphasises how, in the social world we live in, others often do evaluate us by considering whether we comply with those kinds of principles. By either following or violating those principles, we also create certain expectations in others, expectations which they will take into account when they decide how they interact with us later on. By conforming to the non-rejectable principles, we can thus create an atmosphere of trust around us. Such atmosphere can lead to mutually beneficial co-operation in the future, which will also then be in our more selfish interests. Furthermore, if we fail to follow the non-rejectable principles, others are bound to hold us responsible for not regarding them as someone to whom justification is owed. As a consequence, they are likely to distance themselves from us, which will be a concrete loss.[11]

3 Objections to Scanlon's Contractualism

After the outline of Scanlon's contractualism in Section 2, this third section focusses on the most important objections to the view. These objections outlined in the subsequent subsections argue that Scanlon's view (1) leads to implausible moral consequences in the so-called aggregation cases, (2) fails to provide a plausible account of our moral obligations to non-human animals and cognitively limited human beings, (3) cannot support intuitive deontic distinctions and (4) is merely a redundant addition to ethical theorising.

---

relationships, such as friendship, must be grounded in the value of mutual recognition in the first place (160–8).

[11] Scanlon (2008: chap. 4) also uses this idea of how we often distance ourselves from others when they do not take into account our reasonable objections to give an account of what blame comprises.

Before we proceed, I want to emphasise that there are also other interesting objections to contractualism.[12] The objections discussed here are merely the most often discussed ones. Secondly, Scanlon himself already tried to address all four objections in *What We Owe to Each Other*.[13] The discussions of these objections have, since 1998, therefore mainly focussed on trying to explain why his attempts to address these concerns were not successful. Furthermore, since 1998, both Scanlon and many others have tried to develop new contractualist responses to the objections discussed in what follows. This section will not, however, go through any of these responses as I return to them in Section 5.4. That section suggests that, in a more general contractualist framework, the debates concerning this section's objections should be understood as internal debates concerning which version of contractualism is most plausible.

3.1 Aggregation

The basic thought behind the so-called aggregation objection is that, insofar as Scanlon makes right and wrong a function of *personal* objections to different principles, his view leads to implausible conclusions with respect to how different-sized groups should be treated.[14] Three kinds of cases are used to illustrate this problem.

Let us first consider the same harm cases (230). Imagine that you could easily save either one drowning person from one sinking boat or five drowning people from another but you could not do both. Intuitively, here we ought to save as many people as we can: the five rather than the one. However, if we compare pairwise the one person's personal objection to the 'Save Many!' principle to any one of the five individuals' personal objections to the 'Save One!' principle, these objections seem equally strong. This is why it does not seem like contractualism could vindicate the intuitively correct 'Save Many!' principle as the non-rejectable principle.

Furthermore, consider a principle according to which, in the previous case, we ought to hold some form of a lottery to decide what to do (Timmermann, 2004). It seems like the strongest objection anyone could make to this principle (receiving a certain probability of dying) is weaker than the strongest personal

---

[12] These objections have, for example, argued that Scanlon's view is too demanding (Ashford, 2003), committed to an objectionable form of generalism (Dancy, 2004), unable to explain the strength of our moral reasons (Mendus, 2003) and leads to either indeterminacy or relativism (Timmons, 2003). I assume that, like the objections discussed here, these objections are also good objections to some versions of contractualism but not to others (see Section 5).

[13] For aggregation, see (229–41); for non-human animals and cognitively limited human beings, see (177–87); for deontic distinctions, see (81–6 and 106–7); and, for redundancy, see (215–18).

[14] See, e.g., Doggett (2009), Hooker (2003: 69–75), Norcross (2002), Otsuka (2000), Parfit (2003), Raz (2003), Reibetanz (1998) and Timmermann (2004).

objections which the relevant individuals could make to the 'Save Many!' and 'Save One!' principles (certain death). As a result, Scanlon's contractualism seems to entail that the right thing to do in the same harm cases is to hold a lottery, whereas it would be wrong to save as many people as you can. Many people take this to be an absurd consequence of the view.

Let us then consider the different harm cases. In the first example of this type of case, you can save either one person's life or a large number of people from loss of a limb, blindness or paralysis (239). Intuitively, here too we should save the larger group, at least when it is big enough. Yet the objection which the one individual can make to the 'Save Many!' principle (certain death) is stronger than any of the personal objections which the members of the larger group could make (loss of a limb, blindness, paralysis) to the 'Save One!' principle. Because of this, Scanlon's contractualism seems to make the latter principle non-rejectable and thus requires saving the one person from death. Again, many would regard this to be an implausible consequence of the view.

Derek Parfit (2003: 380–1) asks us to consider a slightly different case. Imagine that an individual called Blue and a large group of people suffer from a disease that will cause them 100 weeks of pain if we do nothing. We can either help Blue, in which case he will feel no pain at all (and the members of the group will still each suffer for 100 weeks), or help the large group, in which case its members will only suffer for 90 weeks (whereas Blue will still suffer for 100 weeks). Parfit claims that, if the group is large enough, we want to say that we should help the members of the large group to avoid 10 weeks of pain each rather than Blue to avoid all the 100 weeks of pain. He argues that Scanlon's contractualism cannot entail this conclusion no matter how many people there are in the group because Blue's personal reason to reject the 'Save Many!' principle will always outweigh the group members' personal objections to saving him.

Finally, let us consider the social risk imposition cases. The following example is from Johann Frick (2015: 181–2):

> *Mass Vaccination (Unknown Victims)*: One million young children are threa-
> tened by a terrible virus, which is certain to kill all of them if we do nothing.
> We must choose between mass producing one of the two vaccines . . .:
>
> • Vaccine 1 is certain to save every child's life. However, . . . [i]f a child
>   receives Vaccine 1, the virus is certain to paralyse one of the child's legs
>   [permanently] . . .
> • Vaccine 2 . . . gives every child a 999/1,000 chance of surviving the virus
>   completely unharmed. However, for every child, there is a 1/1,000 chance

that Vaccine 2 will be completely ineffective and that the child will be killed by the virus ...

Whichever of the two vaccines we choose to produce will be administered to all one million children.

In this situation, we could adopt either the 'Produce Vaccine 1!' principle or the 'Produce Vaccine 2!' principle. Intuitively, the latter principle is the correct one as we would rather take the risk that some children will die than know that one leg of every child will be paralysed.

The problem is that Scanlon's contractualism seems unable to vindicate this intuition. According to it, we first need to consider what kind of standpoints the previous principles create for different individuals. We know that the 'Produce Vaccine 1!' principle will entail one million saved lives even if all the individuals who will live these lives will have to suffer the harm of a paralysed leg. In contrast, the 'Produce Vaccine 2!' principle leads to 999,000 saved, paralysis-free lives and 1,000 lives that are cut short. We then need to compare the personal objections which the individuals who would live under these principles would have to them. Here, it is evident that the personal objections to the 'Produce Vaccine 1!' principle (paralysed leg) would be weaker than the personal objections to the 'Produce Vaccine 2!' principle (early death). As a consequence, the former principle would be non-rejectable and thus, according to Scanlon's contractualism, producing Vaccine 1 would be the right thing to do. Again, many people would reject the theory for this reason.

3.2 Non-Human Animals and Cognitively Limited Human Beings

We have certain obligations with regards to how we are to treat both non-human animals and cognitively limited human beings (such as seriously mentally disabled adults and infants). There are many things it would be wrong to do to the members of these groups and we have excellent reasons for avoiding those actions. For example, it is clearly wrong to make non-human animals and cognitively limited human beings suffer just for the sake of it. The second major objection to Scanlon's contractualism is that the view seems unable to explain just why that would be the case.[15]

Recall that, according to Scanlon, the key reason why we should do right actions is that, by doing so, we can recognise other people's ability to evaluate reasons, which in turn enables us to form valuable moral relationships of mutual recognition. However, non-human animals and many cognitively limited

---

[15] See, e.g., Hills (2010: 240), Hooker (2000: 66–70), Kymlicka (1990), Nussbaum (2006) and Phillips (1998).

human beings cannot evaluate reasons and, as a result, they lack the relevant kind of rationality needed for recognising the abilities others have for evaluating reasons. For this reason, we simply cannot form relationships of mutual recognition with non-human animals, severely mentally disabled people or infants. Scanlon's theory thus seems unable to explain why we should not wrong the members of these groups.

Secondly, in Scanlon's view, what is right and wrong is a function of how strong the reasons different individuals have for objecting to different moral principles are. Yet many philosophers have thought that having a reason for doing something requires an ability to act in that way.[16] One reason for accepting this principle is that it is natural to understand reasons as considerations that count in favour of only those attitudes (and actions) that are sensitive to our judgements about reasons (20). If the previous general principle is correct, then having a reason to object to a moral principle also requires being able to object to that principle. Without the ability to do any objecting, you just could not have a reason to object. As a consequence, because non-human animals and cognitively limited human beings lack the capacities required for making objections to moral principles, they could not be said to have any reasons for doing so either. Yet, if this were right, then whichever actions are right and wrong according to Scanlon's contractualism would be a function of only the reasons that cognitively capable human beings have for objecting to different moral principles. Hence, whatever consequences moral principles have for non-human animals and cognitively limited human beings, they do not seem to bear on what is right and wrong at all according to Scanlon's view.

Let us consider a principle that would permit boiling a dog alive just because you felt like doing so. The previous considerations seem to entail that no dog could reasonably reject this principle because no dog could have a reason for making an objection to it. This threatens to entail that, according to Scanlon's contractualism, there is nothing wrong with the horrendous action in question. Here, someone might argue that at least dog lovers could reject the previous principle because its adoption would burden them (222). They would, after all, suffer from knowing that some of the dogs they love so much would die in a horrible way. Yet this response to the challenge is not very compelling (Hooker, 2000: 68). This is because intuitively we think that non-human animals and cognitively limited human beings matter not merely because we care about them but also more directly in their own right. Many of us believe that they have a moral status: they are a genuine source of moral obligations in themselves.

---

[16] For a list of defenders and a recent defence, see Streumer (2007).

3.3 Deontic Distinctions

The third objection claims that Scanlon's contractualism fails to support the so-called deontic distinctions.[17] We can approach these distinctions from two famous thought experiments:

> *Transplant* (Thomson, 1976: 206): David is a great transplant surgeon. Five of his patients need new parts – one needs a heart, the others need, respectively, a liver, stomach, spleen and spinal cord – but all are of the same, relatively rare, blood type. By chance, David learns of a healthy specimen with that very blood type. David can then take the healthy specimen's parts, killing him, and install them in his patients, saving them. Or he can refrain from taking the healthy specimen's parts, letting his patients die.

> *Strategic Bomber vs. Terror Bomber* (Bratman, 1987: 139–40): Both Terror Bomber and Strategic Bomber have the goal of promoting the war effort against Enemy. Each intends to pursue this goal by weakening Enemy, and each intends to do that by dropping bombs. Terror Bomber's plan is to bomb the school in Enemy's territory, thereby killing children of Enemy and terrorizing Enemy's population. Strategic Bomber's plan is different. He plans to bomb Enemy's munitions plant, thereby undermining Enemy's war effort. Strategic Bomber also knows, however, that next to the munitions plant is a school, and that when he bombs the plant he will also destroy the school, killing the children inside. Strategic Bomber has not ignored this fact. Indeed, he has worried a lot about it. Still, he has concluded that this cost, though significant, is outweighed by the contribution that would be made to the war effort by the destruction of the munitions plant.

Many people believe that, in *Transplant*, David should not save the five patients by killing the healthy specimen. Likewise, many people think that the Terror Bomber is doing something wrong, whereas the Strategic Bomber is not. These intuitions seem to support the so-called deontic distinctions. They suggest that there are things we should not do (or intend to do) even when doing so would have good consequences overall. The ends do not justify the means.

Various deontic principles are often used to explain our intuitions about the previous cases. The defenders of the doctrine of doing and allowing, for example, argue that there is an important moral difference between killing and letting die: killing someone is a much worse thing to do than merely letting a person die. If true, this principle would explain why David is not allowed to sacrifice the healthy specimen. He would be killing him, whereas he only has to let the other five die. Likewise, the defenders of the doctrine of double effect

---

[17] See, e.g., Brand-Ballard (2004) and Kamm (2007: 470–4).

argue that there is an important moral difference between intending something bad to come about and merely foreseeing that the same outcome will materialise through one's agency. The former is again supposed to be much worse than the latter. Roughly, this doctrine states that, if you are pursuing a worthwhile end, you are allowed in some cases to act in ways that cause a foreseeable harm even if you would not be allowed to intend to bring about the same harm in a similar case. If true, this principle would explain the moral difference between the Strategic Bomber and the Terror Bomber. Both are pursuing the same good outcome but the latter is intending to bring about certain harms, whereas the former merely foresees that those harms will be an unavoidable side effect of otherwise good actions.

Scanlon's contractualism seems unable to support our intuitive verdicts about the previous cases. It also seems to fail to vindicate the more general deontic principles behind them. In both cases, we should again begin from different principles that could govern cases like these. In *Transplant*, we could adopt either the 'Do nothing!' principle or the 'Save five by killing one!' principle. We then need to consider what kind of burdensome standpoints the general adoption of these principles would create for different individuals. The problem is that the most serious personal objections to these two principles again seem to be just as strong. The 'Do nothing!' principle will lead to the deaths of five individuals, whereas the 'Save five by killing one!' principle will require the healthy specimen to bear exactly the same burden. This is why Scanlon's contractualism seems unable to explain why the intuitively correct 'Do nothing!' principle in this case would be non-rejectable. It does not seem like there would be more serious personal objections to all other principles. As a result, contractualism seems unable to explain why David should not kill the healthy specimen and thus the view also seems unable to support the doctrine of doing and allowing in this context.

Similar things can be said about the second case. Here, we need to consider four potential principles: one that authorises strategic bombing, one that forbids it, one that authorises terror bombing and one that forbids it. Let us begin from comparing the first two of those principles first. We can assume that there is some contractualist explanation of why the principle that forbids strategic bombing can be reasonably rejected, whereas the principle that permits it cannot be. Perhaps this is because, if strategic bombing were forbidden, this would lead to more horrific wars and that would cause some individuals the kind of serious personal burdens that no one would have to experience if strategic bombing were permitted.

However, if this contractualist rationale is able to justify strategic bombing, it can also be applied to terror bombing. This is because terror bombing has exactly the same consequences as strategic bombing to all individuals. Both can make wars shorter and thus save lives and prevent other burdens. Furthermore, both can even cause exactly the same burdens to the same individuals. After all, the only difference between the actions is the intention with which they are done. Otherwise their consequences are exactly the same. As a consequence, if one of these practices is authorised/forbidden by the non-rejectable principles, so must the other be too. This is why Scanlon's contractualism does not seem to entail that terror bombing would be more wrong than strategic bombing and, as a result, it also does not seem to be able to vindicate the doctrine of double effect in this context.

3.4 Redundancy

Perhaps the most often repeated objection to Scanlon's contractualism is the so-called redundancy objection.[18] This section follows Nicholas Southwood's (2009: 934–44; 2010: chap. 7) way of distinguishing between different versions of the concern. I will only add one additional form of purported redundancy to Southwood's list.

3.4.1 Explanatory Backwardness

Scanlon's contractualism tries to explain what is right and wrong in terms of the non-rejectable principles. One of the earliest critics, Judith Jarvis Thomson, already argued that Scanlon's view therefore gets the order of explanation the wrong way around (Thomson, 1990: 30, fn. 19):

> My impression is that the explanation goes in the opposite direction – that it is the patent wrongfulness of the conduct that explains why there would be general agreement to disallow ... [the relevant type of actions].

Because the deontic restriction (see Section 2.1) is built into the formulation of reasonable rejectability in Scanlon's contractualism, according to this view the wrongness of an action can never count as a reason to reject a moral principle. However, Thomson feels like such reasons should be accepted. Is she right?

Thomson is right to argue that, if we accept that the wrongness of an act can be a reason to reject a principle that permits it, we cannot use the non-rejectable principles to explain which actions are right and wrong. Doing so would be viciously circular: wrongness of actions would explain reasonable rejectability and reasonable rejectability would explain wrongness.

---

[18] Seven years after the publication of *What We Owe to Each Other* more than fifteen philosophers had already made this type of objection to Scanlon's view. For references, see Suikkanen (2005: 40, fn. 2).

Do we then have any good reasons for excluding the wrongness of actions from the reasons to reject a principle? I believe we do *insofar as we aim* to give a substantial non-circular explanation of right and wrong; and, when we explicitly exclude such reasons, the resulting version of contractualism cannot be circular at least in the direct way just explained (it can still be circular in some other way however). It is, of course, a different question of how good the resulting contractualist explanation of right and wrong is. This depends on how well the contractualists can defend their view against different objections and how good the other potential explanations of right and wrong are in comparison. Yet, whatever turns out to be the best explanation of which actions are right and wrong, Scanlon's contractualism cannot be accused of explanatory backwardness. Scanlon cannot be required to give up the aim of explaining what is right and wrong and for that reason he cannot reasonably be asked to give up the deontic restriction either.

3.4.2 Explanatory Inferiority and Redundancy

The second redundancy objection claims that, even if Scanlon's view provides a potential explanation of right and wrong, there are always better explanations available. This objection is clearly stated by Colin McGinn (1999: 36):

> Why is it wrong to cause unnecessary pain to infants and animals? Is it
> because they could reasonably object to such treatment? Hardly . . . Surely
> the reason it is wrong to cause non-rational beings pain is that pain is a bad
> thing, and hence it is wrong to cause it for no good reason.

Here, McGinn makes two claims (see Southwood, 2010: 177). He first assumes that causing pain to infants and animals is wrong either because it is forbidden by a non-rejectable principle or because pain is bad. He then claims that the latter explanation of the relevant action's wrongness is better than the former, and so it turns out that contractualism is not a plausible explanation of why actions are wrong.

The critics of contractualism can also explain why there are always better explanations available. This is because the non-rejectable principles themselves are a result of the very same moral considerations that can explain right and wrong more directly. As Simon Blackburn (1999) puts it:

> Suppose that it is reasonable to reject my principles because, for instance,
> they lead to vast inequalities of wealth. Why isn't this the feature that makes
> my principles wrong? Why go through the detour of dragging in the hypothe-
> tical agreement with others?

Thus, whenever some individuals are able to reject certain principles because the actions they permit burden them in certain ways, these burdens themselves are already sufficient to make the actions in question wrong. As a consequence, the non-rejectable principles are never really needed for explaining what is right and wrong.

3.4.3 Explanatory Circularity

The third version of the objection claims that, when we rely on the non-rejectable principles to explain right and wrong, this explanation will implicitly rely on our pre-theoretical moral convictions. This makes the contractualist explanation circular and, as a consequence, unable to justify our pre-theoretical moral convictions in any meaningful sense. Brad Hooker (2003: 58) formulates the concern in the following way:

> Suppose contractualists say not only that wrongness is determined by principles that no one could reasonably reject but also that those whose rejection of principles matters are those who recognise such-and-such moral distinctions and who have such-and-such moral priorities, etc. In this case, it is not that moral distinctions are being determined by what reasonable contractors agree to, but rather that moral distinctions are determining what counts as a reasonable contractor. Moral distinctions are serving as input to the contract, rather than its output.

In the formulation of his contractualism, Scanlon stipulated that you could only reasonably reject a principle if you have certain motivations. You must be 'moved to find principles for the general regulation of behaviour that others, similarly motivated, could not reasonably reject' (4). Thus, without the previous motivations, your objections to a given principle will simply not count for the reasonable rejectability of the principle. Hooker's concern is that, once we begin to limit the individuals whose objections matter in this way, we will bring in our prior convictions of which actions are right and our view becomes circular as a result.

Here is a simple illustration. Let us return to the intuition that there is a moral difference between killing and letting die (see Section 3.3). We could stipulate that all reasonable contractors whose objections will count must recognise this distinction. The consequence of this could well be that no one could reasonably reject the principles that recognise a moral difference between doing and allowing. No one would have a reason to object to such principles, as anyone who would potentially have an objection would already be excluded. Yet, in this case, the critics of contractualism would be right: the moral difference between killing and letting die has merely been taken for granted rather than vindicated.

3.4.4 Explanatory Non-fundamentality

In Scanlon's contractualism, the notion of reasons plays a fundamental role. Reasons themselves are often taken to be a fundamental normative notion that cannot be explained in any other normative terms (17; see also Schroeder, 2005). Reasons can roughly be understood as considerations that count in favour of different attitudes and actions. The central element of this way of understanding reasons is the normative 'being a reason for' or 'counting in favour of' relation between the considerations that are the reasons and the actions and attitudes they support.

Scanlon's contractualism, then, relies on reasons in two important places. Firstly, the non-rejectable principles are a function of how strong the personal reasons individuals have for objecting to different principles are. Secondly, the reasons we have for following the non-rejectable principles equally play an important role.

Southwood (2010: 73), then, objects that this reliance on reasons makes contractualism *explanatorily non-fundamental*:

> the role of Scanlon's contractors consists in tracking reasons that are prior to and independent of their decisions to accept and reject particular principles. Far from the contractors having absolute authority to determine what is right, it is in virtue of the contract-independent reasons and their weight that contractors accept and reject particular principles. If normative reality were different – if some individuals' reasons counted for more than others', say – then the contractors would accept and reject different principles. Scanlon's Kantian contractual situation is parasitic on more fundamental normative considerations. It is in virtue of these more fundamental normative considerations that we have the particular moral obligations we do. Reasonable rejectability within Scanlon's Kantian contractual situation is explanatorily non-fundamental: it does not provide us with an ultimate grounding of morality.

This passage contains two objections. It first suggests that the whole notion of a contract and what the contractors do does not work in Scanlon's theory. This is because the contractors have no 'absolute authority' but rather the rightness and wrongness of actions are determined solely by their reasons. The second objection is that, because which moral principles could not be reasonably rejected is a function of reasons, these reasons must be the fundamental grounding of morality rather than the non-rejectable principles. Thus, even if the contractualist explanation of rightness and wrongness proceeds via the non-rejectable principles, ultimately this explanation bottoms out at the level of the more fundamental reasons. This is why they would be more important than the non-rejectable principles.

3.4.5 Motivational Redundancy

Finally, I will add one more redundancy objection to Southwood's list.[19] Many people have read Scanlon to be claiming that we must refer to the non-rejectable principles to explain what reasons we have for doing the right thing. According to this reading, these reasons are based on the valuable moral relationships we can form by following those principles, the relationships of mutual recognition. Many critics have then argued that these reasons are redundant – we already have more concrete, sufficiently strong reasons to do the right thing prior to any moral relationships of mutual recognition.

Consider Scanlon's case against utilitarianism (152). He begins from the feeling of disgust he felt when reading Peter Singer's (1972) 'Famine, Affluence, and Morality'. Scanlon felt bad because people were starving in Bangladesh and also because of how wrong it was for him not to be helping those people. Scanlon's point here is that this kind of concrete moral disgust could not be explained if wrongdoing were merely a matter of failing to follow an abstract principle that requires us to maximise the general good.

Scanlon's own theory, however, seems to suffer from the same problem. It seems difficult to accept that Scanlon was disgusted at himself because he failed to follow the non-rejectable principles and thereby value other people's capacity to evaluate reasons. A much more attractive explanation would begin from concrete first-order considerations such as that there are people suffering and I am not helping them. This explanation suggests that the best reason Scanlon really had for helping people in Bangladesh was their suffering rather than any morally valuable relationships of mutual recognition which Scanlon could form. This seems to entail that Scanlon's account of what reasons we have for doing right actions is redundant. There are already always much simpler reasons to do right actions than the more abstract reasons based on the relationships of mutual recognition.

4 The Consequentialising Project

4.1 From Classical Utilitarianism to the Consequentialist Framework

Before we turn to how contractualists have tried to address the previous objections, this section first briefly considers the recent changes in how contractualism's main competitor, consequentialism, is understood as a theory. It has become evident that we should draw a distinction between consequentialism understood as a general framework for ethical theorising and different versions

---

[19] See, e.g., Stratton-Lake (2003: 74–6) and Wallace (2002: 455).

of consequentialism. This section describes what led to this re-evaluation of consequentialism. Section 5.1 then argues that we should, likewise, draw a distinction between contractualism understood as a general framework for ethical theorising and different versions of contractualism. Most of Section 5 then explores the consequences of this new way of understanding contractualism.

The historical origin of consequentialism is, of course, classical utilitarianism. Its founding fathers, Bentham and Mill, were both hedonists (Bentham, 1789/1996; Mill, 1861/1998). They thought that the only thing that has value/ disvalue is pleasure/pain. Following them, we can call the balance of pleasure and pain a person's level of happiness. Bentham and Mill's utilitarianism then argued, very roughly, that right actions maximise the amount of general happiness, whereas wrong actions fail to do so.[20]

As an ethical theory, classical utilitarianism then entails that certain specific actions are right and wrong. The most famous objections to utilitarianism, after all, use different problem cases to attack the first-order ethical implications of the view. If the right thing to do is to maximise the amount of general happiness, then in *Transplant* (see Section 3.3) we should save the five by killing the healthy specimen. Likewise, assuming classical utilitarianism, we should hand over an innocent person to a lynch mob demanding justice, be a satisfied pig rather than a dissatisfied human being, create as many people as possible as long as their lives contain more pleasure than pain and break our promises, give up our personal projects and not be faithful to our loved ones.[21]

The previous objections have given rise to more sophisticated consequentialist theories, which try to avoid the problematic implications of classical utilitarianism by changing some elements of the theory. The resulting theories keep the core element of utilitarianism, according to which an action's rightness always depends on how good its consequences are. This is why these views are still forms of consequentialism. These views have, however, often rejected classical utilitarianism's theory of value, hedonism. The thought was that, with more sophisticated axiologies, we can avoid the previous objections to classical utilitarianism. This is what motivated John Stuart Mill (1861/1998: 2.3–9) to draw the distinction between lower and higher pleasures and G. E. Moore (1903) to formulate his version of ideal consequentialism, according to which outcomes should no longer be evaluated in terms of how much general happiness they contain but rather in terms of how good they are, full stop.

---

[20] Since Urmson (1953), however, it has been more common to interpret Mill as a rule-utilitarian.
[21] In the order of the objections, see, e.g., McCloskey (1965), Carlyle (1850/1885), Parfit (1984: chap. 17) and Ross (1930/2002: 37–9).

Since Mill and Moore, the number of different versions of consequentialism has proliferated. This leads to an interesting question: what makes an ethical theory a version of consequentialism? I believe that all versions of consequentialism must have a certain structure. This is why, generally speaking, consequentialism should be understood as a framework in which different ethical theories can be formulated. The structure of all versions of consequentialism can be captured in terms of the following three elements:[22]

1. An option set element: when an agent is in a choice situation, all versions of consequentialism must assign the agent some set of options.
2. A theory of value element: all forms of consequentialism must then include a theory of value that can be used to evaluatively rank the agent's options in terms of how good their consequences are.
3. A deontic function element: all forms of consequentialism must finally define how what is right and wrong is a function of the previous evaluative ranking of the agent's options.

We can then see how classical utilitarianism is just one version of consequentialism that shares the same structure with other versions of consequentialism. The classical utilitarians assumed that an agent's options in a situation consist of all the mutually exclusive actions that the agent could do. They then argued that the general balance of pleasure and pain can be used to evaluatively rank the outcomes of the agent's options. The option that produces most happiness overall is ranked first and then the remaining options are ranked lower the less general happiness their consequences contain. Finally, the classical utilitarians' deontic function was a maximising one. They thought that only the action that is ranked first in the evaluative ranking is right, whereas all other actions are wrong.

Yet, if we keep the classical utilitarianism's consequentialist structure but make changes to the option set, theory of value and deontic function elements, we end up with very different versions of consequentialism that authorise and forbid very different actions. For example, a version of consequentialism according to which, instead of pleasure, we should maximise the perfection of human capabilities will not consider the same actions to be right and wrong as classical utilitarianism. Likewise, a view according to which right actions merely need to have good-enough consequences will permit many actions which classical utilitarians would regard as wrong.

When the flexibility of the consequentialist framework became evident, many philosophers started to pursue a new project. It was realised that there

---

[22] See, e.g., Dreier (2011: 97) and Smith (2003: 576; 2009: sec. 1).

are hardly any limits to the ways in which the option set, theory of value and deontic function elements of consequentialism can be formulated and so there will be a vast, perhaps infinite number of different versions of consequentialism. This thought gave rise to a hypothesis now known as the Extensional Equivalence Thesis (EET) (Dreier, 2011: 98). According to it, whichever plausible moral view we take, there will be a version of consequentialism that is extensionally equivalent to it. This is to say that, whichever actions you believe to be right or wrong, it is possible to formulate the three elements of consequentialism in such a way that we end up with a version of consequentialism that agrees with you about which actions are right and wrong. The attempt to show that EET is true has become known as the consequentialising project.[23]

4.2 The Consequentialising Project and the Key Move

Different people's ethical views, of course, take different types of actions to be right and wrong. Many people think that it is wrong to lie or break a promise. Others might think that it is wrong to type thank-you notes or eat meat. How can we then formulate versions of consequentialism that agree with these different ethical views?

One key assumption of classical utilitarianism is that, when determining whether a given action is right or wrong, we should focus only on the *causal* consequences of the action, on whether people will be happy after the action as a result of it.[24] This is why classical utilitarianism entails that it is right to break a promise when this brings about more general happiness than keeping the promise.

The key move in the consequentialising project is to reject the previous assumption (Dreier, 2011, 98–9). If we do so, we can understand the fact that a certain type of action has been done as one of the consequences of an action. As a result, one outcome of telling a lie will be that a lie has been told. This is not a causal consequence of the action but rather its *constitutive* consequence. Furthermore, the theory of value element of consequentialism can also be formulated so that outcomes can be better or worse merely in virtue of whether

---

[23] For an overview, see Portmore (2009). For defences, see, e.g., Dreier (1993, 2011), Louise (2004), Portmore (2007, 2011) and Suikkanen (2009, 2014a). For objections, see, e.g., Brown (2011) and Schroeder (2007).

[24] The notion of 'causal consequences' has to be read very broadly here. If I fail to give a life-saving medicine to someone who is about to die, it could be argued that, in a narrow sense, my inaction does not cause the person to die but rather that it was her illness. Yet the person's death in this case is one of the consequences of my inaction which the utilitarians would take into account. Here, however, whether or not I give the medicine to the dying person makes a difference to how things will turn out for that person. This means that, in a broader sense, the person's death can be considered to be one of the causal consequences of my inaction (even if that death might not be caused by my inaction in the strictest sense).

they contain the doings of certain kinds of actions. One theory of value might, for example, claim that the mere fact that a promise has been broken can itself make an outcome of an action bad, whereas another might stipulate that the mere fact that a thank-you note has been written by hand makes an outcome better.

If these two moves are allowed, then it is easy to formulate different versions of consequentialism corresponding to different ethical views. If your ethical view forbids breaking promises, your version of consequentialism should assign the consequence that a promise has been broken enough disvalue so as to make promise-breaking always wrong. Likewise, if your ethical view requires that thank-you notes must be written by hand, then the axiological element of your version of consequentialism should highly value the outcome that a thank-you note has been written by hand. This is how the previous key move enables us to formulate different versions of consequentialism that all correspond to different ethical views concerning which actions are right and wrong.

The previous key move is not, however, enough for consequentialising all ethical views. This is because some ethical views have structural features that prevent them from being consequentialised in the previous simple way. I will next discuss three such structural features: agent-centred constraints, agent-centred prerogatives and moral dilemmas.

4.2.1 Agent-Centred Constraints

Ethical views committed to constraints hold that there are some actions that you should not do even if they had the best consequences. Consider a situation in which you can either do nothing, in which case C will kill five innocent people, or kill B, an innocent bystander, in which case C will get distracted which will enable the five other innocents to escape. Many people believe that, in this situation, you should not kill B even if doing so would have the best consequences. After all, by sacrificing B, you could save four more innocent individuals from being killed in exactly the same way.

The problem is that the key move just described will not help us to formulate a version of consequentialism according to which you should not kill B. Even if we make the fact that an innocent person is not killed a good-making feature of outcomes, the outcome in which you kill B will still be better. After all, five innocent people are not killed rather than just one innocent person. Because of this, it was quickly noticed that the only way to accommodate constraints is to adopt an agent-relative theory of value. This is the idea that *relative to you* the outcome in which you kill one innocent person can be worse than the outcome in which C kills five people (even if from an agent-neutral perspective the latter outcome is better). This is because the former agent-relative value ranking can take into account your own agential involvement – the fact that *you* would be doing the killing – whereas, from the perspective of an impartial spectator, the fact that you would be doing the killing rather than C makes no difference.

If we then add that, for each agent, right actions bring about the best outcomes relative to them, we get different versions of consequentialism that can recognise constraints. These consequentialist views will sometimes require agents to do actions that do not have the best consequences from the agent-neutral perspective. In the previous case, for example, they would claim that I ought not to kill B because not doing so brings about the best outcome relative to me even if this outcome will not be the best according to the agent-neutral evaluative rankings.

At this point, Mark Schroeder (2007) has objected that, even if the previous proposal does the trick in theory, it should not be accepted unless we can explain what it would mean for an outcome to be good relative to an agent. This explanation should furthermore make sense of the fundamental consequentialist requirement that we bring about as much value as possible. In response, Douglas Portmore (2007) has suggested that we can make sense of agent-relative value by relying on a fitting-attitude account of value. His thought is that to be good relative to me is to be what it is fitting for me to value. It could then be thought that what is agent-neutrally good is what, for an impartial spectator, would be fitting to value (Suikkanen, 2009). As a result, the outcome in which I have killed B is bad relative to me because it is not fitting for me to value the outcome in which I have killed an innocent person. In contrast, for an impartial spectator it is fitting to value this outcome because, even if I end up killing B, five other innocent people are saved from being killed by C. This is why a fitting-attitude theory of both agent-relative and agent-neutral value can enable us to formulate a version of consequentialism according to which it is wrong for me to do certain things even if they would make things go best in agent-neutral terms.

4.2.2 Agent-Centred Prerogatives

In addition to constraints, many of us are also committed to agent-centred prerogatives: freedoms to do things that do not have the best consequences. Imagine that you wake up early on a Saturday morning. You could stay in bed, or get up and have some breakfast, or watch television, or go for a run. However, you could also use your computer to donate all your money to an online charity or get the first bus to volunteer at the local homeless shelter. According to classical utilitarianism, if one of these options produces more general happiness than the rest, then only that option is permissible, whereas all other options are wrong. Intuitively, however, we would think that, if you did any of the previous things, you would not do anything wrong.

How could we formulate a version of consequentialism that could match our intuitions about the previous example? Let me introduce two simple ways to do this.[25] The first option is to reject the maximising part of the deontic function element of classical utilitarianism. The so-called satisficing versions of consequentialism claim that right actions need not have the best consequences but rather it is enough if the actions in question have good-enough consequences (Slote, 1982; Vallentyne, 2006). The defenders of this view can then give an account of what counts as good-enough either (1) absolutely in terms of a threshold which the value of the consequences of a given action must exceed or (2) proportionally by specifying how close the value of the consequences of a given suboptimal action must be to the value of the best option. Either way, according to the resulting versions of consequentialism, agents will often have intuitive moral freedom to do actions that do not have the best consequences.

The second simple way to accommodate agent-centred prerogatives in the consequentialist framework is to move from act-consequentialism to rule-consequentialism. Rule-consequentialist theories begin by evaluating different sets of moral principles, moral codes, in terms of how good the consequences of their general internalisation would be (Hooker, 2000). Such theories then argue that an action is right if and only if it is authorised by the moral code the general adoption of which would have the best consequences. In the case of agent-centred prerogatives, rule-consequentialists can stipulate that one potential outcome of the adoption of a moral code can be that the code leaves room for autonomy and freedom to make choices between many different permissible options. They can also claim that this consequence itself can make the outcome of a code good. On this basis, rule-consequentialists can argue that there are agent-centred prerogatives to do suboptimal actions because the adoption of a moral code that gives us such prerogatives would have the best consequences (Mulgan, 2006: 165).

---

[25] In Suikkanen (2014a), I also go through the other ways in which agent-centred prerogatives can be consequentialised, including strategies based on hybrid views (Scheffler, 1982), coarse-grained axiologies and dual-ranking (Portmore, 2011: chap. 11). In the same article, I also outline a new proposal, according to which act-consequentialists too could rely on the value of freedom.

4.2.3 Moral Dilemmas

Peter Vallentyne (1989: 301) has used a simple example to introduce two types
of moral dilemmas. Imagine that Smith promises to call his wife at 5 p.m. but
then forgets this promise. He then also promises to call Jones exactly at the same
time. Of course, he cannot keep both promises. In this case, some people have
the intuition that, no matter what Jones does, he will do something wrong. Their
views are committed to the existence of prohibition dilemmas – situations in
which all alternatives are wrong. Some people also believe that Smith ought to
call his wife at 5 p.m. and he also ought to call Jones at the same time. They are
committed to the existence of obligation dilemmas – situations in which there
are many mutually exclusive actions you ought to do.

Classical utilitarianism does not leave room for the previous kinds of dilemmas. In every situation, there will be either one or several options that have
better consequences than all the other alternatives. Classical utilitarianism
entails that these options must be permissible and so, according to it, there
cannot be situations in which all options are wrong. Similarly, classical utilitarianism also rules out situations in which you would be required to do many
mutually exclusive actions. If there is only one option that has better consequences than all other alternatives, then only that option is required. When there
are many equally best options, according to classical utilitarianism you are
permitted to choose any one of them. Because of this, according to classical
utilitarianism, neither prohibition nor obligation dilemmas exist.

It is, however, again possible to formulate the option set, theory of value
and deontic function elements of consequentialism so that we will get
versions of consequentialism according to which there are both types of
dilemmas. Let me just outline one way of doing so. Consequentialists who
want to accommodate moral dilemmas can begin from theories of value that
contain value incomparability (Dreier, 2011: 105–7). Let us assume that, in
the previous example, the value of the outcome of Smith calling his wife
and the value of the outcome of Smith calling Jones cannot be compared.
This is to say that it is not the case that one of these outcomes is better than
the other nor is it the case that they are equally good (Chang, 1997: 4).
Rather, the value of these outcomes just cannot be compared – exactly in
the same way as we find it difficult to say whether it would be better to be
a successful accountant or a struggling dentist (Raz, 1986: 342).

Let us then consider a version of consequentialism according to which an
option is permissible if and only if it has better consequences than all other
options. If we assume in the previous example that the outcomes of Smith
calling his wife and Smith calling Jones cannot be compared and ranked, then in

this situation there is no option that would have better consequences than all other alternatives. As a result, this version of consequentialism entails that no action Smith could do would be permissible. This version of consequentialism thus entails that there are prohibition dilemmas. A version of consequentialism could also stipulate that an option is required if and only if the value of its outcome cannot be evaluatively ranked with respect to the outcomes of the agent's other alternatives. According to this view, because the outcome of Smith calling his wife and the outcome of Smith calling Jones cannot be ranked with respect to one another, both options would be required. This version of consequentialism would thus be able to accommodate obligation dilemmas.[26]

4.3 The Key Methodological Promise

This section has suggested that consequentialism should be understood as a flexible framework, as a structure in which different versions of consequentialism can be formulated. We have seen that this enables us to formulate versions of consequentialism that correspond to different plausible ethical views. The key move allows us to create versions of consequentialism that fit different views of what kind of actions are right and wrong. The key move itself will not enable us to accommodate certain structural features of our moral views, but we have also seen how those structural features too can be accommodated in the consequentialist framework. This is why EET continues to seem plausible: whatever plausible ethical view we take, it looks like we can create a version of consequentialism that is extensionally equivalent to it.

The question then is: why should we create all these different versions of consequentialism in the consequentialist framework? There are at least two good reasons. Firstly, from a consequentialist perspective, the fact that we have all these versions of consequentialism makes the consequentialist framework itself immune to first-order ethical objections. These objections turn out to be objections to specific versions of consequentialism but not to the consequentialist framework.

Let me illustrate this by returning to H. J. McCloskey's (1965: 256) famous counterexample to classical utilitarianism. You are a sheriff of a small town in which a white woman has been raped. You do not know who committed the crime but everyone is angry. People are so angry in fact that, if you do not do something quickly, there will be rioting and many people will die. In this case, one option you have is to hand over an innocent bystander to the mob. One person will die in this case, but many more will be saved too. According to

---

[26] For a more thorough discussion of different ways to consequentialise moral dilemmas, see Suikkanen (forthcoming).

classical utilitarianism, you ought to maximise the amount of general happiness and so in this case you should let the innocent bystander be murdered.

This example is an effective objection to classical utilitarianism. Yet the tools introduced in Section 4.2 enable us to formulate versions of consequentialism that can easily avoid the problem. For example, we could adopt a theory of value according to which an innocent person being punished for a crime they did not commit makes the outcome a lot worse. If this is right, then not handing the bystander to the mob will have the best consequences. Even if people do die in the resulting riots, according to the proposed theory of value, this need not be as bad as the murder of the innocent person for a crime they did not commit. Thus, even if this case is a counterexample to classical utilitarianism, it cannot be a counterexample to more sophisticated versions of consequentialism.

Exactly the same move can be made in the case of all the famous counter-examples to classical utilitarianism. All those examples argue that classical utilitarianism has implausible first-order ethical consequences in certain cases. The flexible framework of consequentialism allows us, however, to formulate different versions of consequentialism that can accommodate the common-sense intuitions on which the objections are based. This is why, as a consequence of the consequentialising project, the traditional disagreement between the defenders of classical utilitarianism and its critics can now be translated into a disagreement concerning which version of consequentialism is correct. Is it classical utilitarianism or some other version of consequentialism that can better match our moral intuitions about different cases? We have therefore been able to transform the traditional objections to classical utilitarianism into internal debates concerning which version of consequentialism is correct.

The second benefit we get from creating all these versions of consequentialism is what Jamie Dreier (2011: 114–17) has called the key methodological promise of the consequentialising project. Dreier's thought is that, by creating a version of consequentialism that is extensionally equivalent to a given ethical view, we can translate that view to the language of consequentialism. The promise, then, is that this translation will make the view's structural features and evaluative commitments clearer. We can see what elements of outcomes the view takes to have intrinsic value, whether its value theory is agent-relative or deontic function satisficing and so on. The hope is that, once these features of different ethical views have been made more transparent through the versions of consequentialism that correspond to them, it will provide us with new means to evaluate how plausible the relevant ethical views are overall. Instead of continuing to trade conflicting intuitions, we will now have something more fundamental to rely on when we consider what kind of ethical views we should accept.

5 The Contractualist Framework

Section 4 outlined fascinating recent developments in the world of consequentialism. These discoveries will now enable us to understand contractualism in a new way. Section 5.1 explains how we should also draw a distinction between the general framework of contractualism and different versions of contractualism (such as Scanlon's contractualism) that can be formulated in that framework. Drawing this distinction will have many benefits. First of all, it will allow us to understand what is common to all versions of contractualism and how contractualist theories in general differ from consequentialist theories. As Section 5.2 will show, it will also enable us to map more clearly the differences between the different versions of contractualism that have been recently discussed in the literature.

Drawing this distinction will, however, also have more radical benefits. Firstly, as outlined in Section 5.4, it will allow us to transform different objections to Scanlon's contractualism (see Section 3) and the contractualist responses to them into internal debates about which version of contractualism is correct. In this way, contractualism too will become immune to counterexamples. Section 5.3 will, in addition, argue that the contractualist framework is just as flexible as the consequentialist one: for every plausible ethical view, there will also be a version of contractualism that is co-extensive with it. As a consequence, a further benefit of the new way of understanding contractualism will be the promise that, because we can translate different ethical views also to the language of contractualism, this too will provide us with new ways of evaluating the plausibility of different ethical views.

5.1 The General Contractualist Structure Versus Different Versions of Contractualism

Section 4 explained how, when Bentham and Mill invented classical utilitarianism, they actually did two things. They both (1) introduced a general consequentialist structure consisting of an option set, a theory of value and a deontic function and (2) created a specific utilitarian version of consequentialism by formulating those structural elements of consequentialism in a certain way. Of course, the forefathers of utilitarianism did the former without explicitly intending to do so. The general structure of the consequentialist views only became evident later on through the process in which the critics of classical utilitarianism presented counterexamples to the view and others tried to respond to those objections by developing new versions of consequentialism. This allowed philosophers to extract the abstract structure which all consequentialist views share.

This subsection argues that, when Scanlon introduced his contractualism, he too did two things.[27] He both (1) introduced a general contractualist structure and (2) created a specific version of contractualism by formulating the structural features of contractualism in a certain way. At the moment, on the basis of different objections to Scanlon's contractualism (see Section 3), new versions of contractualism that share the more general structure of contractualism are beginning to emerge. This is why we now need to distinguish the structural elements of contractualism from Scanlon's version in the same way as the similar distinction was drawn in the case of consequentialism. The rest of this subsection suggests that contractualist theories have four structural elements: an option set element, a comparison base element, a normative ranking element and a deontic function element. Formulating these elements in different ways then generates different versions of contractualism, including Scanlon's own version.

5.1.1 The Option Set Element

Just like the consequentialist theories, all forms of contractualism require some set of options to compare. In Scanlon's version of contractualism (see Section 2.1), these options are always individual moral principles that could govern certain kinds of situations – a certain domain of behaviour. We should compare all the potential principles that could govern promise-keeping, or the ones that could govern helping others, telling the truth, killing and so on. When we compare the principles that could govern a certain domain of actions, we hold the other moral principles fixed. This is because, in the comparisons of one type of principles, individuals can rely on other principles in the reasonable rejection of the relevant candidates.

However, individual principles governing a certain domain of actions are not the only alternatives that the contractualists could compare. Let me introduce two other ways to formulate the option set element. Firstly, instead of comparing individual principles in a certain domain, contractualists could compare whole moral codes – different all-encompassing sets of different moral principles – at the same time (see Hooker 2003: 62–6). I believe that we should, actually, prefer this formulation of the option set element to

---

[27] Scanlon's work was, of course, inspired by a long tradition of contractualist thought, especially in political philosophy. This tradition goes back from Rawls (1972) all the way to Hobbes (1651/1996), Locke (1689/2002) and Rousseau (1762/1997).

Scanlon's own view on contractualist grounds for the following reason. Image that we go through Scanlon's procedure. We first select a non-rejectable moral principle for one domain whilst holding the other principles fixed. We then select a non-rejectable moral principle for a different domain whilst again holding others fixed (now including the previous non-rejectable principle) and then we keep repeating the procedure until we arrive at a stable set. Imagine that we also select separately a whole non-rejectable set of all moral principles directly by comparing the personal burdens which all the different possible complete moral principle sets create for different individuals (and here we assume that individuals can only reasonably reject these sets on the basis of burdens that are not based on any particularly moral principles).

Two things could happen in this case. Either the two sets of moral principles arrived at in the two different ways would be the same or they would be different. If they were the same, then Scanlon's way of comparing individual principles one domain at a time would be redundant. We could arrive at the same result also more directly. If they were different, then the set of moral principles arrived at through Scanlon's procedure would cause some very serious personal burdens to some individuals such that no one would have to experience similar burdens under the set of principles arrived at via the second procedure. After all, that procedure compared all possible sets of moral principles and arrived at the non-rejectable set by comparing which set causes the least serious personal burdens. This is why the option set element of contractualism should be formulated in terms of whole sets of moral principles rather than individual domain-specific principles.

There is, however, a third alternative: act-contractualism (Sheinman, 2011). Instead of individual moral principles or whole moral codes, the contractualists could compare all the particular actions that a given agent could do in the situation they are in. We could consider what kind of personal standpoints these different actions would create for different individuals and compare the actions in this option set others could reasonably reject. The non-rejectable action in a given situation would be such that there would be more serious personal objections to all other alternatives – all of them would burden some individuals in more serious ways.

Any contractualist theory must thus contain an option set element. However, we get different versions of contractualism when we formulate that element in different ways – be it in terms of individual principles, sets of principles, possible actions in a given situation, motivations, characters or something else.

5.1.2 The Comparison Base Element

After the option sets, all forms of contractualism must introduce something on the basis of which those options can be compared. Scanlon actually told us

surprisingly little about how his version of contractualism formulates this
element; but perhaps a formulation of this element can be extracted from the
following sentence: 'In order to decide whether this is so [whether a principle
permitting one to do X could be reasonably rejected], we first need to form an
idea of the burdens that would be imposed on some people in such a situation if
others were permitted to do X' (195).[28] My reading of this sentence is that, when
we compare different principles that could govern a domain, we do this by
comparing the consequences that the general adoption of those principles will
have for different individuals. We can thus think that every option in the
specified option set is paired with a certain possible world.

For example, if we compare different sets of principles, we pair each set with
a world in which that code has been internalised. These worlds are exactly like
the actual world in terms of their natural resources, human abilities and so on
except that everyone accepts a different set of moral principles within them.[29]
The idea, then, is that, because different sets of moral principles have been
accepted in these worlds, individuals come to think and behave in different
ways in them, which will in turn influence the kinds of lives people come to live.
The different lives, which different individuals will come to live in these worlds,
then provide us with a basis for comparing which one of the moral codes could
not be reasonably rejected. Likewise, similar sets of worlds to be compared can
also be generated if the relevant options are individual principles or actions.

Here too, however, there is room for different versions of contractualism.
Scanlon seems to suggest that we compare the consequences of *everyone*
accepting a certain principle for governing a certain domain of actions. This,
unfortunately, would be problematic for two reasons. Firstly, consider the
principle 'Do not be violent unless some other people endorse violent rules, in
which case kill as many people as you can!' (see Parfit 2011: 315–16). If
everyone accepts this rule, it has no harmful consequences and so perhaps it
could not be reasonably rejected. However, in the real world where not everyone accepts non-violent moral principles, following the previous rule would
have disastrous consequences. This is why the non-rejectable principles, which
also determine which actions are right here in the actual world, should not be
a function of what would happen if everyone accepted certain principles.

Secondly, we also want contractualism to be able to generate principles that
could govern moral education and disagreeing with others (see Hooker 2000:
80–5). However, if we assume that principles are compared at the 100 per cent
level of social acceptance, then any such principles could be reasonably

---

[28] See also 202–5 for Scanlon's discussion of standpoints.

[29] In John Rawls's (1972: 126–30) words, the options are thus compared in the 'circumstances of
justice'.

rejected. After all, in the 100 per cent acceptance worlds, the principles that would require us to teach our moral views to others or not solve our moral disagreements with violence would be completely redundant and so only impose unnecessary costs on everyone. Thus, if we want our duties of moral inculcation and disagreement to be justified on the basis of the non-rejectable principles, these principles should be compared in worlds in which not everyone accepts the same moral principles. In those worlds, different inculcation and disagreement principles would make a genuine difference to people's lives and so some would be more burdensome than others.

The lesson of this is that we must compare different options in the contractualist framework at a level lower than 100 per cent of acceptance; and, here too, we get different versions of contractualism depending on what we take that level to be. It could be suggested that we should compare the options (1) at a set level (say, 90 per cent of acceptance), (2) at every level or (3) at a certain equilibrium level characteristic for a given set of principles given how demanding the inculcation element of the code is.[30] We also get different comparison bases depending on what kind of counter-culture we take those individuals who do not accept the moral code of a given world to have (for a discussion, see Suikkanen 2017).

5.1.3 The Normative Ranking Element

Contractualists will then need to produce a certain kind of ranking of the options in light of the comparison bases. At this point, it is important to note that this ranking cannot be *an evaluative ranking*. The ranking in question cannot be generated by how good the comparison bases of the different options are, that is, it cannot be a comparison of how much value these comparison bases contain. This is because otherwise contractualism would collapse into consequentialism (see Section 4.1).

Because of this, one key difference between consequentialism and contractualism at the most general level is that contractualist ethical theories must rank the relevant options in terms of their comparison bases *normatively*.[31] The

---

[30] Option (1) is defended by Hooker (2000: 80–5), option (2) by Parfit (2011: 317–19) and Ridge (2006) and option (3) by Smith (2010) and Suikkanen (2014b). Parfit claims that there must be a principle that would be non-rejectable at every level of acceptance, whereas Ridge would appeal here to some form of average burdensomeness for an individual when every level of social acceptance is taken into account.

[31] This is not to say that consequentialism, as the view was described in Section 4, is not a normative view. Consequentialists, for example, argue that we ought to do whatever has the best consequences where that 'ought' is very much a normative one. It's just that, at this crucial point, consequentialists compare the relevant options in evaluative terms – in terms of how much value their consequences contain.

relevant ranking must be produced by relying on the strength of reasons or on some other normative notions such as 'rationality', 'ought' or the like. Because of this, in order to generate the required kind of normative ranking of the relevant options, contractualists must formulate a first-order theory of some normative notion, which they can then use for ranking the relevant options on the basis of their comparison bases.

We can then start from Scanlon's own formulation of the normative ranking element. As it has become evident, Scanlon's normative ranking relies on the core normative notion of reasons. Yet Scanlon also describes a certain view of whose reasons for doing what are relevant in the evaluation of different principles. We are to compare the personal reasons that different individuals living under different moral principles have for making objections to the principles under which they live. Finally, and most importantly, Scanlon also gives a rough description of these reasons – of what the relevant considerations are on the basis of which objections can be made and of how strong the resulting objections are.

According to Scanlon (204), the relevant reasons must be *generic reasons* that are not based on the individual's particular aims, preferences, tastes or other personal characteristics. They must also be personal reasons based only on the qualities of the objector's own life (219). These reasons can be based on the consequences of a given principle to the individual's level of well-being but they can also be based on other concrete considerations that make one's life more or less choice-worthy. Furthermore, these considerations include moral considerations based on the other moral principles that are not compared in the given example. As already mentioned in Section 2.1, Scanlon (204) gave the following list of examples of the kinds of reasons that count: bodily harms, not being able to rely on the assurances of others and not having control over what happens to one's own body. Through Scanlon's examples, a picture also emerges of how strong he thought different reasons for rejecting principles are.

Let us then change some elements of Scanlon's normative theory. Imagine that we, for example, stipulate that the reasons for making objections must be based only on the effects which the relevant principles have on our own level of well-being or that we also allow impersonal reasons for rejecting principles.[32] In both cases, given that the non-rejectable principles are a function of the reasons recognised by our normative theory, different moral principles will become non-rejectable. This is why even the smallest changes to Scanlon's formulation of the normative ranking element of his version of contractualism

---

[32] The former stipulation is defended by Reibetanz (1998: 311 fn. 18); the latter by Parfit (2003).

will lead to different versions of contractualism, according to which different actions are right and wrong.

This means that, just as we can generate different versions of consequentialism by relying on different kinds of theories of value, we can similarly generate different versions of contractualism by relying on different normative theories. Contractualists can formulate different versions of contractualism (1) by relying on other normative notions than reasons, (2) by comparing some other reasons than personal reasons to reject principles and (3) by formulating different first-order normative views concerning which considerations count as the relevant reasons and how strong the reasons those considerations provide. Sections 5.2–5.4 will suggest next that, because there can be so many different normative rankings of the relevant options, the general contractualist framework turns out to be incredibly flexible. In fact, it turns out to be exactly as flexible as the consequentialist framework.

5.1.4 The Deontic Function Element

The last, deontic function element of Scanlon's own version of contractualism is simple. It states that we are to first pick out the moral principles that are ranked first in the previous normative ranking, that is, the non-rejectable principles. All the actions that these principles authorise are then right and all the actions that are forbidden by them are wrong.

We should, however, recognise that there also exists other ways to get from the previous normative rankings of the options to which actions are right and wrong. Let me use act-contractualism as an illustration (see Section 5.1.1). Take all the actions that an agent could do in a certain situation. These options can then be ranked in terms of how strong different individuals' personal objections would be to these actions on the basis of how these actions would burden them. One 'satisficing' version of act-contractualism could then state that an action is permissible if and only if it is highly enough ranked in the previous normative ranking. This would be either when the most serious objections to the action are not much more serious than the most serious objections to the highest ranked action or when the most serious objections to it do not exceed a certain absolute threshold of seriousness.

Similar satisficing versions of contractualism could also be formulated when we compare different moral principles or sets of moral principles. It could be, for example, stipulated that an action is permitted if it is authorised by at least one of the highly enough ranked moral principles and wrong otherwise. It is thus possible to generate different versions of contractualism by varying how we get from the normative ranking of the relevant options to right and wrong actions. This is exactly in the same way as we get different versions of consequentialism depending on how we get from the evaluative rankings of options to right and wrong actions. The consequentialists have already started to explore what consequences making use of this leeway will have (see Section 4.2.2) and so there is no reason why the contractualists could not do so too.

5.2 Other Versions of Contractualism in the Literature

Section 5.1 drew a distinction between the general structure of contractualism and different versions of contractualism that share that structure. I suggested that the contractualist framework, as a structure, consists of four elements: an option set, a comparison base, a normative ranking and a deontic function. I then explained how Scanlon's own version of contractualism formulates each one of these elements. The key point, however, was that, when we formulate the four elements of contractualism in different ways, we get different versions of contractualism as a result. This section, then, briefly introduces three other versions of contractualism that already exist in the literature. These contractualist views can now be formulated in the more general contractualist framework described in Section 5.1. One advantage of doing this is that we can be more precise about just how these contractualist views differ from Scanlon's contractualism.

5.2.1 Parfit's Kantian Contractualism

In *On What Matters*, Derek Parfit (2011: sec. 49) introduced a version of Kantian contractualism, which he thought could be defended as the supreme principle of morality. Parfit believed that this theory, which is loosely based on Kant's Formula of Universal Law formulation of the Categorical Imperative, could avoid all the serious objections to all other Kantian principles and their different interpretations. This section explains how Parfit's view can be understood as a version of contractualism in the general framework spelled out in Section 5.1. It is a view that has the same structural elements as Scanlon's contractualism even if it formulates those elements in a different way. The key difference between these two views is how they specify the normative ranking element of contractualism.

Parfit (2011: 341) formulates his Kantian contractualism by beginning from a principle called the 'Formula of Universally Willable Principles':

> An act is wrong unless such acts are permitted by some principle whose universal acceptance everyone could rationally will.

Let me then unpack this principle. The relevant moral principles of this formula have been *universally* accepted when *everyone* accepts them. Universal acceptance, furthermore, requires both (1) that everyone believes that the given principles are correct and (2) that everyone is disposed not to do acts that are forbidden by those principles just for that reason.

Parfit (2011: 356) uses the term 'willing' in the previous principle in a technical sense. We are to imagine that everyone has a magical power to determine which moral principles everyone else accepts. Given this power, when an agent wills the universal acceptance of some principles, they *see to it* that everyone accepts them. When could you then rationally see to it that something is the case? According to Parfit's (2011: 111) view, rationality is a matter of responding to good reasons correctly by coming to have the attitudes that those reasons require. This entails that, when we consider whether you could rationally will that something is the case, we must begin from the state of affairs you would be willing to obtain. Following Parfit (2011: 45), if a given state of affairs itself provides reasons to will its obtaining, then that state of affairs provides you with 'object-given' reasons to will its obtaining. You can then rationally will a certain state of affairs to obtain when the qualities of that state of affairs provide you with sufficient object-given reasons for seeing to it that it will obtain. Sufficient reasons for doing something are, furthermore, not decisively outweighed by reasons for doing anything else.

This entails that whether you could rationally will the universal acceptance of certain principles depends on whether the circumstances in which everyone accepts those principles have some qualities that would provide you with sufficient reasons for seeing to it that those principles would be universally accepted. That everyone could rationally will the universal acceptance of some principles thus requires that the qualities of the state of affairs created by the universal acceptance of these principles provide sufficient reasons for everyone for seeing to it that everyone accepts those principles.

When we consider whether everyone would have sufficient reason to see to it that everyone accepts certain moral principles, we image each person separately standing outside our world with their special power of determining what moral beliefs everyone has in our world. We then ask each person at a time whether they could rationally will that every person accepts the given principles within our world. This is required because one cannot imagine a world within which everyone has simultaneously the power of deciding which moral principles everyone accepts (Rosen, 2009: 83). We can then restate Parfit's Kantian contractualism like this:

An act is wrong if and only if it is forbidden by the principles that everyone
has sufficient reasons for seeing to it that everyone accepts.

Let me then explain how this view's formulation of the normative ranking
element of contractualism differs from Scanlon's formulation of that element.
Firstly, even if the initial formulation of Parfit's view seems to rely on a different
normative notion – on rationality rather than reasons – this is not a genuine
difference between the views, because Parfit understands rationality in terms of
reasons. Secondly, the key difference between the views is that Scanlon's view
is formulated in terms of reasons to reject principles, whereas Parfit's view is
formulated in terms of what principles everyone has reasons to see to it that
everyone accepts. This difference is important for the following reason.

According to Scanlon's view, when we consider which principles could not
be reasonably rejected, we only take into account certain very specific reasons.
We only consider the reasons each individual has for objecting to the principles
under which they live. Of these reasons, we then only take into account the ones
that are based on the objector's standpoint's burdensome qualities for which
those principles are responsible. This constraint thus makes explicit the individualist restriction on the relevant reasons. In contrast, Parfit's theory takes into
account a larger variety of different kinds of reasons. This is because, when it
comes to which principles everyone has sufficient reason for seeing to it that
everyone accepts, these reasons include *all the reasons* given to every individual by the states of affairs in which the different principles are accepted. Thus,
for example, the fact that many people would suffer under a certain principle
gives me (and everyone else too) an impersonal, agent-neutral reason not to see
to it that everyone accepts that principle. This explains why Parfit's Kantian
formulation of the normative ranking element does not include the same
individualist restriction as Scanlon's contractualism.

A second difference is that, in Scanlon's view, the wrongness of actions is
a function of only the strongest personal reasons of those who are burdened
most by the different principles. In contrast, in Parfit's view, an act gets to be
wrong only if every person has sufficient reasons to see to it that everyone
accepts the principles forbidding it. In this situation, we take into account not
only the strongest reasons which some individuals have but rather all the
reasons of all individuals. According to this view, it might turn out that
a certain act is wrong in part only because some individuals have only relatively
weak reasons to accept the principle forbidding the act.

Parfit's Kantian contractualism thus formulates the normative ranking element of contractualism in a very different way. Yet Parfit's view is also still
flexible. His abstract formulation of the normative ranking element is still

compatible with very different first-order normative theories of reasons. In Parfit's framework, such views lead to different views of which principles individuals have sufficient reason to see to it that everyone accepts. This means that, if we combine different first-order theories of reasons with Parfit's abstract principle, we get very different versions of contractualism: different views of which actions are right and wrong. This allows Parfit (2011: 411–12) to even argue that, despite the structural differences between his own version of Kantian contractualism and Scanlon's contractualism, these theories are still extensionally equivalent – they can authorise and forbid exactly the same actions.

5.2.2 Southwood's Deliberative Contractualism

Whereas Parfit only seemingly relies on the notion of rationality in his formulation of the normative ranking element, Nicholas Southwood's (2010, 2019) version of contractualism does so explicitly. This is because, as we saw in Section 3.4.4, according to Southwood, if we rely on reasons to formulate the normative ranking element of contractualism, this threatens to make contractualism explanatorily non-fundamental in an objectionable way. As a consequence, Southwood relies on the notion of rationality instead. His version of contractualism states that (Southwood, 2019: 531):

> It is morally impermissible/obligatory for A to X [if and only] if we were all perfectly deliberatively rational and charged with the task of agreeing upon a common code by which to live, then we would agree to live by a common code, C, that includes principle P that forbids/requires A to X.

Let me then unpack Southwood's view too. Firstly, Southwood (2019: 531) stipulates that the 'we' in the previous schema refers to every human being who is deliberatively competent. Secondly, the schema directs us to consider a hypothetical situation in which we all are given a certain task (Southwood, 2010: 102; 2019: 532). We are to agree upon which shared moral code we are to live by where this would require internalising the code and thereby complying with it and also holding others to account with respect to its principles.

Finally, and most importantly, in the hypothetical situation we are considering we are all made deliberatively fully rational (Southwood 2010: 88–96 and 2019: 532). In this scenario, we would thus all be making decisions on the basis of prolonged deliberation subject to three kinds of deliberative norms. The first, communicative norms, require that we are sincere, intelligible and open during the co-deliberation. The second, discursive norms, govern the rational ways in which we are to persuade one another with arguments and they also require that we are open to being persuaded by others in similar ways. The third, reflective norms, require that we make our own beliefs, desires and other mental states coherent and unified and also that we modify these attitudes in the light of the co-deliberation. These norms furthermore require us to have a high degree of self-acquaintance or, otherwise, frank exchanges with others would not be possible.

Southwood's version of contractualism then claims that a normative ranking of different moral codes can be created by considering how we would all rank the possible moral codes as an output of the previous kind of idealised rational deliberation. The code we would all agree to live by would be ranked first, our second choice second and so forth. What is right and wrong for us to do in the real world is then, in Southwood's view, a function of which actions the moral code ranked first would forbid and permit.

When ranking different moral codes normatively, Southwood's view thus does not rely on reasons at all. Rather, the relevant ranking of moral codes is generated by the formulation of the principles of deliberative rationality and what we all would agree on if we were made deliberatively rational in the ways specified by those principles. Yet, given that rationality itself is arguably a normative notion, the ranking generated through Southwood's procedure is also a normative ranking rather than an evaluative ranking.[33] This is why Southwood's theory shares the general contractualist structure outlined in Section 5.1. This is the case even if his version of contractualism formulates the normative ranking element in a unique way. It should also be noted that, like Parfit's theory, Southwood's theory also could be used to generate many different, more specific first-order versions of contractualism. This is because the norms of deliberative rationality could be formulated in different ways.

5.2.3 Gauthier's Contractarianism

Let me finish this section by explaining how a well-known version of contractualism called 'contractarianism' can also be formulated within the general contractualist framework.[34] This theory has its origins in Hobbes's (1651/1996) social contract theory but today it is usually discussed on the basis of David Gauthier's (1986) formulation of the view. Gauthier's theory can here be understood as a distinctive formulation of the normative ranking element of contractualism.

Gauthier (1986: chap. 2) begins from a simple conception of rationality according to which rational agents choose alternatives that maximise the

---

[33] For an overview of the debate on the question of whether rationality is normative, see Kiesewetter (2017).

[34] For a more thorough overview of contractarian views, see Moehler (2020).

satisfaction of their own interests where what is in their interests is determined by their considered and coherent non-instrumental desires and preferences. Basically, according to this view, rational choice is merely a matter of getting what you really want.

In the present framework, Gauthier's contractarianism can be understood as the view that moral codes can be ranked normatively in terms of how rational it would be for everyone to accept them. It thus generates a normative ranking of the relevant options (the moral codes) on the basis of the normative notion of rationality understood in the traditional decision theoretic way. Gauthier also argues that there must be a unique moral code, which it would be most rational for every individual to internalise. Why would this be the case? He answers this question in two stages.

Gauthier (1986, chap. 6) first explains why every rational agent would choose to adopt some moral principles to constrain their pursuit of their selfish interests. For example, consider the principle that requires us to keep our agreements. Is it rational for you to adopt that principle? Let us assume that you live in a community in which others tend to keep their agreements. We can then imagine that you have just made an agreement with one member of your community. This agreement requires you to do something for the benefit of the other person but you can also expect that it will benefit you in turn in accordance with what you have agreed. If we think of just this case, you might think that the rational thing for you to do would be to not keep your part of the deal. You would still receive the benefit from the other person's contribution without having to sacrifice any of your own interests for the sake of benefitting them.

Yet, if you do not keep your part of the agreement, this will become common knowledge and, thereafter, others in the community will no longer make agreements with you; and, if this happened, you would lose out – you would no longer be able to make mutually beneficial agreements but rather you would be on your own. Because the previous long-term benefits outweigh any benefits you could gain by not keeping your agreement in an individual case, it is in your selfish interests to adopt a general policy that requires you to stick to what you have agreed to do. Similar explanations can also be given for why it is rational to internalise many other traditional moral principles. These arguments themselves do not, however, determine exactly which moral principles it would be rational for every individual to accept. This is also a problem because many different co-operative arrangements based on different moral codes are available and different codes benefit some people more than others. How do we know whether there even is a unique code that would be most rational for everyone to accept?

According to Gauthier (1986: chap. 5), the content of that unique moral code must be an outcome of a bargaining process. He argues that, during this bargaining process, every rational agent would adopt what he calls the 'Principle of Minimax Relative Concession'. Imagine that we are setting up a co-operative venture. Its outcome will consist of both each person's individual contribution and an additional 'social surplus'. The minimum benefit you could then get from the co-operation would be your own contribution but merely getting the benefit would not make the co-operation worthwhile for you. The maximum you could get would, in contrast, be your own contribution plus the entire social surplus. Others would not, however, co-operate with you on those terms. This means that, whilst you would like to get as much of the social surplus as possible, you must make a concession: you must share some of the social surplus with others in order to get them to co-operate. How much would it then be rational for each person in the co-operative venture to concede?

Gauthier (1986: 136) answers this question by first defining the 'relative concession' of each person. For calculating your relative concession, we need three numbers: (1) your initial bargaining position (what you would get if you only got your own contribution: u^*), (2) your claim (what you would get if you got both your contribution and all of the social surplus: $u^{\#}$) and (3) what the outcome is for you after you have made a concession in a given case (u). Your relative concession in a given case then is $(u^{\#} - u)/(u^{\#} - u^*)$. It is how much you end up conceding divided by what your maximum concession could be.

Gauthier's (1986: 137) claim, then, is that rational agents would agree to co-operate according to a principle that would make the maximum relative concession of any person as small as possible. This is still very abstract but the rough idea is that the rational way to divide the social surplus of a co-operative venture is to give each person a part of the social surplus proportionate to their contribution to the co-operative arrangement (Gauthier 1986: 155; see also Smith, 2001: 231). This principle also applies to the choice of moral codes. It is rational for all of us to adopt a moral code such that we benefit from co-operating by following the code in proportion to our contribution to the society. The claim, then, is that the ordinary moral norms that require that we keep our promise, tell the truth and also comply with other forms of fair dealing constitute such a code because following the code consisting of them benefits each individual in proportion to their contributions.

More, of course, could be said about Gauthier's view but here only two observations are in order. Firstly, Gauthier's contractarianism leads to a very different first-order ethical theory than Scanlon's contractualism. One consequence of Gauthier's view is that the moral principles it is rational for everyone to accept will benefit you very little if you cannot make a significant contribution to your society's co-operative ventures: if you are severely disabled or living in abject poverty, for example. In contrast, according to Scanlon's view, a moral principle that burdens non-contributing individuals can still be reasonably rejected by those individuals as long as there are moral principles that do not burden anyone equally seriously.

Secondly, despite such important first-order normative differences, Gauthier's and Scanlon's versions of contractualism still share the same general contractualist structure. They both contain an option set, a comparison base, a normative ranking and a deontic function. The key difference between the views is the different ways in which they formulate the comparison base and normative ranking elements. For Scanlon, the comparison base is what kinds of lives individuals come to live under different principles, whereas, for Gauthier, the comparison base consists of what kinds of divisions of the social surplus different principles create. Likewise, for Scanlon the principles are ranked in terms of how strong the personal reasons different individuals have for objecting to them are, whereas Gauthier ranks the moral codes in terms of how rational it would be for each individual to accept a given division of the social surplus. It is these different formulations of two key structural elements of contractualism that lead Scanlon and Gauthier to very different first-order ethical views.

5.3 How to Create Versions of Contractualism

So far, this section has drawn a distinction between the general contractualist structure and different versions of contractualism. It has also explained how different contractualist theories in the literature can be understood within the general contractualist framework. This section goes on to argue that the contractualist structural framework is just as flexible as the consequentialist framework outlined in Section 4. If this is right, then we have reasons to believe that, for any plausible ethical view, there is also a version of *contractualism* that is co-extensive with it. Section 5.3.1 suggests that, in order to capture different first-order ethical views, contractualists can adopt the consequentialisers' key move (see Section 4.2). The remaining subsections (Sections 5.3.2–5.3.4) then show that there are both (1) versions of contractualism that can accommodate constraints, agent-centred prerogatives and moral dilemmas and (2) versions that correspond to the ethical views that lack those structural features.

5.3.1 The Key Move

Different ethical views require, permit and forbid different actions. Some ethical views might, for example, forbid typing thank-you notes, whereas others permit doing so. The consequentialists' key move for creating different versions of consequentialism that match these different views consists of two steps (see Section 4.2). We first need to include the doings of different types of actions in the constitutive consequences of individual actions. We can then claim that these doings, as elements of the relevant outcomes, can make outcomes better or worse. If you think that the fact that a thank-you note has been typed makes an outcome worse, then your version of consequentialism will usually end up forbidding the typing of thank-you notes. In contrast, if you think that whether a thank-you note has been typed cannot affect the value of an outcome, then your version of consequentialism will usually end up permitting the typing of thank-you notes.

The contractualists can make exactly the same key move in the normative ranking element of their view, that is, in their first-order theory of what reasons individuals have for making objections to different moral principles. If your theory of reasons states that receiving a typed thank-you note is a serious burden, then your version of contractualism will presumably end up forbidding the typing of thank-you notes. Likewise, if your theory of reasons does not take receiving a typed thank-you note to be a burden, then your version of contractualism will end up permitting the typing of such notes; and, just like the consequentialists, the contractualists can make this key move with respect to different types of actions depending on which ethical view they want to capture. This is why there will be different versions of contractualism that correspond to different ethical views that require, permit and forbid different types of actions.

The previous contractualist key move is available exactly for the same reason as the corresponding consequentialist key move. Consequentialists are able to formulate radically different versions of consequentialism by taking both the causal and constitutive consequences of different actions into account in the evaluation of outcomes. Exactly in the same way, contractualists need not take into account only the causal consequences of the adoption of different moral principles but rather they can also consider the constitutive consequences of the adoption of those principles. When considering reasonable rejectability, it is also possible to take into account what kinds of actions are done to different individuals under different moral principles. This move will then allow us to create different versions of contractualism that correspond to different views of what kind of actions are right or wrong.

5.3.2 Constraints

Section 4.2.1 introduced a simple example of constraints. In this example, if I do nothing, C will kill five innocent people. My only alternative is to kill B, which would be enough to distract C so that the five can escape. Should I kill B or not?

This section explains why there is a version of contractualism corresponding to both answers to this question.

Section 3.3 explained why the standard version of Scanlon's contractualism seems to entail that I should kill B in the previous example. This is because that theory compares what would happen to different individuals under the 'Do nothing!' and 'Save five by killing one!' principles. The adoption of the former principle would lead to more people dying than the adoption of the latter principle. As we will see in Section 5.4.1, even if the personal objections which B and each of the five individuals could present to the previous principles would be exactly the same ('my life is cut short'), there are ways for the contractualists to argue that, when the most serious personal objections to two principles are equally strong, the principle under which fewer individuals bear the burden is the non rejectable one. In the previous example, that principle would be the 'Save five by killing one!' principle, which means that, according to this version of contractualism, I should kill B.

There are, however, versions of contractualism that support the 'Do nothing!' principle instead. Such versions of contractualism cannot be merely *patient-centred* (Brand-Ballard, 2004: 275). They cannot compare merely what happens *to different individuals* under different principles but rather they must also contain an *agent-centred* element. They must also take into account what you, as an agent, would have to do under different principles. The first-order normative theory of reasons of one version of contractualism could, for example, state that the burden of having to kill another innocent person – that specific kind of agential involvement – provides you with a very strong reason to reject any principle under which you would be required to kill other innocent human beings. If this consideration is counted as a relevant kind of serious burden – as one that grounds a strong-enough objection – then, according to the resulting form of contractualism, the 'Save five by killing one!' principle could be reasonably rejected, whereas the 'Do nothing!' principle could not be. As a consequence, there are also versions of contractualism that are co-extensive with the ethical views that contain moral constraints – views according to which in the previous example I should not kill B even if this entails C killing five other innocents.

5.3.3 Agent-Centred Prerogatives

It is easy to show that there are versions of contractualism that are compatible with the ethical views according to which we have agent-centred prerogatives. These views claim that we are often permitted to do sub-optimific actions. Thus, even if giving all your money to a charity would have the best consequences of all the actions that you could do when you wake up on a Saturday morning, many ethical views still allow you to stay in bed or at least have breakfast first (see Section 4.2.2).

Creating versions of contractualism that correspond to the previous views is easy. Scanlon (251–6) already argued that his own version of contractualism is one such theory. We again need to begin by comparing the consequences that two different kinds of moral principles would have for different individuals. Let us assume that we could have either principles that in every case give us only one permissible option (perhaps the action that would have the best consequences) or principles that usually give us many permissible options. We can then compare the kinds of lives we all would come to live under these two kinds of principles.

One major advantage of the second type of principles is that they give us quite a bit of freedom – personal leeway to decide what to do in each case. In contrast, the first principles are more burdensome exactly for the reason that they do not give us freedom to make choices. Scanlon (251–3) argues that having such freedom can have at least three different kinds of value: instrumental, representative and symbolic. He thus believes that moral principles that give us freedom are valuable (1) because they enable us to get more of what we want, (2) because by making free choices we can express our attitudes to others (by choosing a certain gift I can, for example, tell my wife that I love her) and (3) because if you are granted freedoms you are recognised as a competent person who can make choices. On this basis, Scanlon then argues that principles that give us little freedom to make sub-optimific choices can be reasonably rejected. Our lives under such principles would be unnecessarily burdensome given that we would lose out on the previous three types of value that result from having moral freedom.

It is, however, also possible to formulate versions of contractualism that do not entail agent-centred prerogatives. This only requires reformulating the normative ranking element of Scanlon's view. As we have just seen, Scanlon's version of contractualism generates agent-centred prerogatives because its first-order normative theory of reasons takes not having freedom to be a good reason to reject a principle. In contrast, if we accepted a theory of reasons according to which not being free is either only a weak reason to reject a principle or no reason at all, then the resulting version of contractualism would entail principles that would not grant us any agent-centred prerogatives. Such versions of contractualism could even lead to moral principles that would always require us to do whatever would have the best consequences.

5.3.4 Moral Dilemmas

Finally, are there versions of contractualism that match the ethical views according to which there are moral dilemmas? In order to answer this question, we must first recognise that the moral codes that are compared in the contractualist framework can contain principles that would entail both prohibition and obligation dilemmas. That is, some of these compared codes could be such that according to them there are both situations in which all options are forbidden and situations in which more than one mutually exclusive option is required.

The question then becomes: is it possible to formulate the normative ranking element of contractualism in such a way that the previous kinds of moral codes could not be reasonably rejected? Let us then return to Peter Vallentyne's (1989: 301) example in which Smith has promised to call both his wife and his friend Jones exactly at the same time. We can then compare the following three principles: principle A which requires Smith to call his wife and prohibits him from calling Jones, principle B which requires Smith to call Jones and prohibits him from calling his wife and principle A&B which requires Smith to call both Jones and his wife at the same time. Because this last principle requires Smith to call his wife, it also forbids him from calling Jones. Likewise, because this last requires Smith to call Jones, it also forbids him from calling his wife. A version of contractualism according to which the principle A&B is the non-rejectable principle would entail that there are both obligation and prohibition dilemmas.

Here is an example of a theory of reasons that would vindicate such a version of contractualism. This theory would have to argue that both principle A and principle B would burden some individuals so much that they could reasonably reject these principles. According to this view, there is an alternative principle A&B that does not create equally serious burdens to anyone. This theory of reasons could, for example, refer to equality. Jones could argue that, because principle A would not require Smith to keep his promise to him, principle A would not grant him an equal moral status as a promisee. Because of this, the principle would fail to respect his equal moral dignity. Smith's wife could, of course, make a similar objection to principle B. Furthermore, this theory would need to add that there is no individual who would be required to experience an equally serious burden under the principle A&B because that principle would treat everyone equally: no matter to whom a promise is made it is always the case that the promise must be kept.

Given that the previous theory of reasons is not completely absurd, it is possible to formulate the normative ranking element in a way that leads to a version of contractualism that recognises both obligation and prohibition dilemmas. It is, of course, similarly possible to formulate versions of contractualism that do not recognise any dilemmas. All you need to do is to formulate a theory of reasons according to which any agent can reasonably reject a dilemma-entailing moral code because such a code will fail to be sufficiently action-guiding, which makes living under the code unnecessarily burdensome.

This section has thus shown that the contractualist framework is just as flexible as the consequentialist framework. Contractualists can borrow the consequentialists' key move to generate different versions of contractualism corresponding to different views of what types of actions are right or wrong. By modifying the normative ranking element of contractualism, we can also create versions of contractualism that can recognise constraints, agent-centred prerogatives and moral dilemmas (and also versions that do not do so). This is why we have reason to believe that, for any plausible ethical view, there must be a version of contractualism that is co-extensive with it.

5.4 From Traditional Objections to Internal Debates

This section returns to the core objections to contractualism discussed in Section 3. These objections can now be understood in a new way. It turns out that the traditional objections to contractualism are all good objections to specific versions of contractualism. Yet there are also other versions of contractualism that match the first-order ethical views that motivate these objections in the first place. This means that the debates concerning these objections should not be understood to be about whether or not contractualism is the correct ethical theory. Rather, they can be understood as internal debates within the general framework of contractualism. What is discussed in these debates turns out to be which form of contractualism is the most plausible one.

5.4.1 Aggregation

Scanlon's contractualism has been argued to fail in three types of aggregation cases (see Section 3.1). It has been claimed that his view fails to explain why we should save the many both in the same harm and in the different harm cases and also that it leads to unintuitive consequences in the social risk imposition cases.

Let me begin from a version of contractualism against which these objections are effective. This version of contractualism has three features. Firstly, it is committed to a strong version of the individualist restriction on the reasons to reject principles. Secondly, it assumes a welfarist theory of the personal reasons to reject principles. These reasons must be based solely on how well or badly off you would be under the given principles. Thirdly, and most importantly, it must be assumed that whether a given principle can be reasonably rejected is to be assessed *ex post*.[35] That is, we consider the worlds in which different principles have been internalised and what kinds of objections individuals in those worlds can make after the consequences of the principles to each individual are clear.

---

[35] *Ex post* contractualism has been defended by Holm (2018), Reibetanz (1998) and Scanlon (1998: 208–9).

If we make these assumptions, then the non-rejectable principles require flipping a coin in the same harm cases, saving the one person from death rather than many from paralysis in the different harm cases and producing Vaccine 1 in the *Mass Vaccination* case. All other principles would lead to more serious burdens given what is counted as a burden.

Yet, if we reject any of the previous assumptions, we get versions of contractualism that have very different consequences. For example, there are versions of contractualism according to which whether a certain principle is reasonably rejectable should be evaluated *ex ante*.[36] This is both before the relevant principles have actually been adopted by everyone and before their consequences to every concrete individual are known. These versions of contractualism put us behind a limited, local and natural veil of ignorance when we consider which principles cannot be reasonably rejected. We will know that the principles will affect a certain number of people in certain ways but we will not yet know which particular individuals will be affected in those ways. From this perspective, the concrete consequences of a certain principle to an individual cannot be that individual's reason to reject the principle given that those consequences do not yet exist. Rather, what we can reject different principles for are the risks they impose on us as individuals. Which principles cannot be reasonably rejected becomes thus a matter of which principles impose unnecessarily serious risks on us.

This version of contractualism has very different ethical implications than the *ex post* version. Let us first compare the risks that would be imposed on individuals by the adoption of the 'Save one!' and the 'Save many!' principles in the same harm cases. We are to consider which one of these principles we could not reasonably reject before we know whether we will end up being the one person to be saved or one of the five people in the group. From this perspective, the 'Save one!' principle would give us roughly a 17 per cent chance of surviving the relevant cases, a flipping a coin principle a 50 per cent chance, a weighted lottery principle roughly a 72 per cent chance and the 'Save many!' principle approximately an 83 per cent chance. Getting an unnecessarily low chance of survival could then be considered to ground an objection to the

---

[36] *Ex ante* versions of contractualism have been defended by Frick (2015), Harsanyi (1975), James (2012), Kumar (2015), Suikkanen (2004) and perhaps also by Scanlon (2013). Furthermore, contractualists can also reject the other assumptions of the above version of contractualism. Thus, Parfit (2003) argues that, if we drop the individualist restriction and accept interpersonally aggregated objections, contractualism can deal with the aggregation cases. Likewise, Scanlon (1998: 229–41) originally argued with the so-called *tiebreak argument* that giving up welfarism about reasons would be enough. He claimed that, in addition to their concrete first-order personal burdens, the members of the larger groups can also object that, unless they are saved, their presence does not make any moral difference, which is a burden in itself. Scanlon also relied on categories of moral seriousness to deal with the different harm cases.

principles that are responsible for it. As a consequence, it could be argued that the 'Save many!' principle is the non-rejectable one. All other principles to govern the situation would impose more serious risks on some individuals from the *ex ante* perspective.

The *ex ante* versions of contractualism can also deal with the other cases in the same way. In the different harm cases, again when we consider which principles could not be reasonably rejected, we do not know whether we will be the one person who might die or one of the many who might be paralysed. We thus need to compare the principle under which no one ever dies even if many become paralysed to a principle that entails that one person dies in each case but always many more will be saved from an almost equally serious harm. Here, it could be argued that, from the *ex ante* perspective, the former principle imposes a more serious risk on every individual. *Ex ante* versions of contractualism can thus entail that the 'Save many!' principles could not be reasonably rejected in the different harm cases either.

What about the original television transmitter case that motivated Scanlon's contractualism in the first place? Isn't there a threat that *ex ante* contractualism fails to provide anti-utilitarian protections in that kind of cases? Well, one *ex ante* version of contractualism could claim that, from the *ex ante* perspective, a guarantee of occasional trivial pleasures does not outweigh the benefit of knowing that you will be saved from very serious burdens when needed. Some *ex ante* versions of contractualism can thus provide anti-utilitarian protections without having any implausible conse-quences in the same harm and different harm cases.[37] Yet other *ex ante* versions of contractualism can claim that, if the chance of trivial pleasures is high enough and the chance of receiving the serious harms small enough, the principle requiring us to save the individuals in cases like the television transmitter case could be reasonably rejected. These versions of contrac-tualism would be extensionally equivalent to the expected value versions of classical utilitarianism.[38]

The *ex ante* versions of contractualism can also deal with the standard social risk imposition cases (Frick, 2015: 187–8). Here, we are to compare from a child's perspective getting a 100 per cent chance of surviving at the cost of a paralysed leg to getting a 999/1,000 chance of surviving (and so also a 1/1,000 chance of dying). Here, it could be argued that, from this perspective, the former risk is a more serious one and thus the principle requiring the production of Vaccine 1 can be reasonably rejected by the individual to whom these risks would be imposed, whereas the alternative that requires Vaccine 2 to be

---

[37] For problems, see Fried (2012) and Frick (2015: 212–23).   [38] See Harsanyi (1975).

produced could not be rejected by anyone. If this is right, then there are versions of contractualism that can lead to plausible principles in these cases too.[39]

5.4.2 Non-human Animals and Cognitively Limited Human Beings

Section 3.2 explained how non-human animals and cognitively limited human beings have been argued to present a problem for Scanlon's contractualism. It has been argued that Scanlon's view can neither explain which actions affecting non-human animals and cognitively limited human beings are wrong nor tell us why we ought not to do those actions. This is because we cannot form relationships of mutual recognition with non-human animals and cognitively limited human beings and because non-human animals and cognitively limited human beings cannot have any reasons to reject principles in the first place.

The previous objections are fair objections to at least some versions of contractualism. The question, however, is: are there versions of contractualism that could avoid them? Let us start with the objection that non-human animals and cognitively limited human beings cannot reasonably reject any principles whatsoever. The thought here is that they cannot have any reasons to make objections to the relevant principles because they lack the cognitive capacities that would be required for doing so. There are at least two ways to avoid this problem.

Firstly, it is possible to formulate a version of contractualism according to which an individual who has to bear a certain burden under a principle does not need to be the same person who makes the objection to that principle that will lead to its reasonable rejection. Scanlon (183) suggested that we could also allow trustees to make objections on behalf of non-human animals and cognitively limited human beings on the basis of their burdens. Perhaps we can think that the trustees can reasonably reject principles on the basis of the personal burdens of others as long as the lives of those other beings can go well or badly. This latter condition is certainly satisfied in the case of non-human animals and cognitively limited human beings.

---

[39] Frick has also argued that there are so-called identified vs. statistical lives cases where not even his version of *ex ante* contractualism can lead to the right conclusions about which actions are right or wrong (Frick 2015: 212–19). He argues that, for this reason, contractualists should accept a form of right-maker pluralism where, in addition to the importance of being able to justify your actions to others on non-rejectable grounds, we also recognise other qualities of actions that can make them right or wrong such as how our actions affect the well-being of others (Frick 2015: 219–23). This is a very different kind of pluralism than the one introduced in Section 6, where I suggest that different ethical theories should be used as deliberation procedures in different kind of cases. For a version of *ex post* contractualism that can deal with the previous cases and also with Frick's identified vs. statistical lives cases without relying on value pluralism, see Suikkanen (2019).

Secondly, we could also adopt a theory of reasons that rejects the principle according to which having a reason for doing something requires the ability to do that action. If we reject this principle, we can think that when the adoption of a moral principle burdens non-human animals and cognitively limited human beings significantly, then those burdens provide a sufficient reason for the non-human animals and cognitively limited human beings themselves to reject the principle in question. Similar burdens would, after all, justify the non-human animals and cognitively limited human beings to make the relevant objections if they were able to do so.

These two formulations of the normative ranking element of contractualism thus create versions of contractualism according to which principles that authorise the mistreatment of non-human animals and cognitively limited human beings could be reasonably rejectable. These versions thus entail that mistreating non-human animals and cognitively limited human beings is wrong. This still leaves us with the second problem: what reason could there be for us to follow the resulting principles if by doing so we cannot form relationships of mutual recognition with the non-human animals and the cognitively limited human beings? In response to this question, it must be emphasised that not all reasons to do the right thing recognised by the contractualists need to be based on the value of mutual recognition (see Sections 2.2 and 5.4.4). There are other reasons to follow the non-rejectable principles.

For example, as already explained, following these principles enables us to avoid causing serious harm to others, including the non-human animals and cognitively limited human beings. Furthermore, by following these principles we can also recognise and respect other qualities than the rationality of others such as their abilities for having sensations, emotions, caring relationships and so on. This means that not all versions of contractualism need to rely on the value of mutual recognition to explain what reasons we have for following the non-rejectable principles. As a consequence, there is hope that these views can describe the reasons we have for also treating non-human animals and cognitively limited human beings well.

5.4.3 Deontic Distinctions

The third objection (see Section 3.3) claimed that Scanlon's view has implausible consequences in the *Transplant* and the *Strategic Bomber vs. Terror Bomber* cases. This objection argues that Scanlon's contractualism fails to vindicate the intuitive deontic principles such as the doctrine of doing and allowing and the doctrine of double effect that are required in those cases.

Let us again grant that there are versions of contractualism to which this is a fair objection. Section 3.3 explained what these versions must be like. We can now, however, also formulate versions of contractualism that entail the doctrine of doing and allowing and the doctrine of double effect. These views would thus lead to the intuitive deontic distinctions in the relevant cases. Here, making the contractualist key move (see Section 5.3.1) is enough.

If contractualists want to recognise the doctrine of doing and allowing, they first need to stipulate in their theory of reasons that the burden of being killed or even harmed by another agent provides you with a strong reason to object to the principles that would allow others to do those things to you. These contractualists will then need to add that the fact that you die or experience harm because others let you die or be harmed does not ground an equally strong objection If this theory of reasons were assumed, then in the *Transplant* case the healthy specimen's objection to the 'Save five by killing one!' principle would outweigh the objections that the five other people would have to the 'Do nothing!' principle.

Likewise, in order to recognise the doctrine of double effect, contractualists only need a theory of reasons according to which having to be the target of another person's intention to kill or harm you is a strong reason to reject the principles that would authorise having that kind of intention. Such intentions could be argued to cause an additional burden to their targets because they would fail to respect their dignity as unique individuals. It could also be argued that, when a person's death is merely a foreseen side effect of someone's action, that person would not be burdened in the same way. According to this theory of reasons, the victims of terror bombing have a stronger reason to reject the principles that permit terror bombing than the victims of strategic bombing have for rejecting the principles that permit strategic bombing. The resulting version of contractualism would thus permit strategic bombing but forbid terror bombing and thereby also recognise the doctrine of double effect at least in this context.

It is thus possible to formulate the normative ranking element of contractualism in ways that lead to versions of contractualism that can recognise the traditional deontic principles behind the intuitive deontic distinctions. This means that it cannot be an objection to the general contractualist framework per se that those principles are correct. Many versions of contractualism will agree with that thought. There is, of course, a further question of whether there really are deontic distinctions and whether the traditional principles behind them are correct. However, within the general contractualist framework, this question can now be understood as an internal question of which version of contractualism is correct.

5.4.4 Redundancy

Finally, let us return to the different versions of the redundancy objection (see Section 3.4). The first, explanatory backwardness problem has already been addressed in Section 3.4.1 and so we can move directly to explanatory inferiority and redundancy. Recall that, according to McGinn (1999: 36) and Blackburn (1999), there are always better explanations of why different actions are wrong than the contractualist explanations based on the non-rejectable principles. Their claim is that the basic considerations such as that certain actions would cause unnecessary pain or lead to vast inequalities of wealth are sufficient to make those actions wrong. This is why being forbidden by the non-rejectable principles would be redundant as a wrong-maker. We also know that the previous type of basic first-order wrong-makers always exist because those very same considerations are required to explain which principles could not be reasonably rejected.

The previous argument, again, is a good objection to some versions of contractualism but not to all. It all depends on the deontic function element of the version of contractualism in question. So far, I have only discussed versions of contractualism that give an account of which actions are right or wrong in terms of the normative ranking of options, that is, in terms of which principles could not be reasonably rejected. When stated in this way, these views are neutral about what *makes* different actions right or wrong: nothing has been said about that matter so far.[40]

We could formulate the deontic function element of contractualism so that we end up with versions of contractualism that are theories of the right-making and wrong-making features. One version of contractualism could state, for example, that the only quality of actions that can make an action right/wrong is the fact that the action is authorised/forbidden by the non-rejectable principles. This view would clearly be vulnerable to the explanatory inferiority and redundancy objections.

Yet there are also versions of contractualism that are not committed to the previous view of the right- and wrong-making features. One version of contractualism could, for example, merely be explicitly a theory of which actions are right or wrong.[41] Such a theory could recognise that the ordinary first-order

---

[40] Of course, many contractualists, including Scanlon, have considered what the right-making features of different actions are. Scanlon's own view is that the very concrete first-order considerations that often consist of different kinds of harms that provide agents with sufficient reasons to reject the moral principles that would allow producing these harms are also the qualities of actions that make them wrong (Scanlon 2004, 136). This fits the version of contractualism described in Section 2.

[41] Alternatively, this theory could also be a theory of the constitution of the properties of rightness and wrongness. See Scanlon (1998: 10–12) and Stratton-Lake (2003).

considerations to which McGinn and Blackburn refer are sufficient right-making and wrong-making qualities of actions in themselves. The defenders of this view could add that their version of contractualism can furthermore explain just why those qualities of actions are able to make the actions that have them right or wrong (Väyrynen, 2013: 171; see also Hieronymi 2011: 106–7). The claim would be that certain first-order features of actions can make them wrong exactly because they are the kind of burdensome features of those actions on the basis of which individuals can reasonably reject the principles that would authorise those kinds of actions.

According to the resulting version of contractualism, McGinn is right to claim that a certain action is wrong because it causes pain to infants and animals. The contractualists can, however, in addition explain why this feature of the action makes it wrong by telling a story of how infants and animals could reasonably reject the principles that would authorise this kind of action precisely because they cause pain to them. Not all versions of contractualism are thus vulnerable to the explanatory inferiority and redundancy problem.

Let us consider explanatory circularity next (see Section 3.4.3). Brad Hooker's (2003: 58) concern is that contractualism becomes viciously circular if we stipulate on the basis of our moral intuitions that a person's objections to a principle do not count unless that person has certain motivations or unless they recognise certain moral distinctions. Here, we can again grant that there are versions of contractualism that are circular in this way. Hooker is right that the versions of contractualism that pick the individuals whose objections count on moral grounds are viciously circular.

Not all versions of contractualism, however, suffer from this problem. All versions of contractualism discussed in this Element have so far been maximally inclusive. They have taken into account the objections of all ordinary human beings and in some cases also the objections that non-human animals and cognitively limited human beings could make to different principles. The versions of contractualism in this Element have thus not set any constraints on the contractors on moral grounds and so the discussed theories cannot have been circular in the way suggested by Hooker.

Perhaps Hooker's concern could be expressed differently. If the key argument of this Element is right, then the general contractualist framework allows us to formulate different versions of contractualism, each one of which takes different actions to be right or wrong. An objection to this would then be that, when we decide which version of contractualism is right, we will have to consult our moral intuitions about cases, and this leads to objectionable circularity.

In response to this concern, we can employ the *companions in guilt* strategy. Section 4 explained how it is also possible to formulate different forms of consequentialism. In this situation, consequentialists – including Hooker (2000: 9–16) himself – are happy to consult their carefully considered moral convictions when deciding which version of consequentialism they should accept. If the consequentialists are then allowed to rely on their moral intuitions in choosing their own versions of consequentialism, the contractualists surely must also be allowed to do the same.

We can then turn to Southwood's objection based on explanatory fundamentality (see Section 3.4.4). His concern is that, in Scanlon's view, reasons play a fundamental role in determining which actions are right or wrong. This leads to two objections: the whole notion of a contract and contractors becomes superfluous and reasons will become the fundamental grounding of morality rather than the non-rejectable principles.

Here, I believe that the contractualists should bite the bullet when it comes to the first concern and rely again on the companions in guilt strategy when it comes to the second. Southwood is correct to point out that, according to the many versions of contractualism which the general contractualist framework allows us to formulate, the notions of contract and contractors play no role at all. Perhaps in this respect the name 'contractualism' is misleading. Section 5.1.3 argued that one key distinguishing feature of all contractualist accounts is that the relevant options are ranked normatively rather than evaluatively. This distinguishing feature has nothing to with contracts or contractors, which explains why many versions of contractualism in my framework will not rely on them at all. Yet, for historical reasons, theories of this type have been called contractualist views and so I too have used that name.

With respect to Southwood's second objection, it is not clear whether it is a problem if, according to a given version of contractualism, reasons play a fundamental role in grounding which actions are right or wrong. Here, contractualists can again appeal to companions in guilt. Firstly, as explained in Section 4.1, all versions of consequentialism have to rely on a theory of value to generate the evaluative rankings of options. If consequentialist views are allowed to do so, then surely contractualists must also be allowed to rely on a prior theory of reasons to generate their normative rankings of options. Furthermore, Southwood himself also relies on a normative notion – that of deliberative rationality – exactly at the same point to generate his normative rankings of options. This means that an objection to his theory too could be that, in his view, the ultimate grounding of morality is rationality. Yet, because these are not serious objections to consequentialism and Southwood's version of contractualism, the fact that Scanlon's view and many other versions of contractualism rely on reasons cannot be a problem either.

Finally, let us briefly consider the motivational redundancy objection (see Section 3.4.5). Here, the concern is that the reasons Scanlon relies on to explain why we ought to do the right thing are redundant. To explain why we ought to be moral, we do not need to refer to the value of the moral relationships of mutual recognition. Rather, all we need to cite are the basic first-order considerations: the reason why we ought to do a certain right action can in one case be that there are people suffering, in another that we would kill someone otherwise or that we have made a promise and so on.

This again seems to be a good objection to some versions of contractualism. If a version of contractualism claims that the *only* reason we have for doing the right thing is that, by following the non-rejectable principles we can form relationships of mutual recognition with other people, then this version of contractualism would be vulnerable to the previous objection. However, there is no reason why other versions of contractualism could not also recognise many other reasons to follow the non-rejectable principles. Section 2.2 thus already explained how even Scanlon's version of contractualism can recognise the first-order reasons we (almost?) always have for following the non-rejectable principles. These reasons are often based on the direct ways in which we would burden others by violating those principles. Scanlon's view can furthermore also recognise many concrete good consequences of complying with the non-rejectable principles. Following these principles can, for example, be argued to create an atmosphere of trust in which mutually beneficial co-operation can flourish.

This means that many versions of contractualism need not emphasise the value of mutual recognition when explaining what reasons we have for following the non-rejectable principles. These versions of contractualism can thus ultimately agree that the reasons based on mutual recognition might in practice be redundant when we try to explain why we ought to be moral.

6 Conclusion

This Element began by outlining T. M. Scanlon's contractualism, which tries to explain both why we should be moral and which actions are right or wrong with one unified theory. It does so by relying on the idea that we have reasons to be able to justify our actions to others on grounds they could not reasonably reject. This starting point enables Scanlon first to argue that the rightness and wrongness of actions is a function of what kind of personal objections individuals can make to different moral principles on the basis of what kind of lives they would live under them. Scanlon can then try to explain why we ought to follow the non-rejectable principles by considering what kind of valuable relationships following these principles enables. He claims that, by complying with the non-rejectable principles, we can recognise other people's standpoints as competent, rational evaluators of reasons. Following these principles thus helps us to form valuable relationships of mutual recognition.

Section 3 then went through some of the most important objections to Scanlon's contractualism. These objections claim that Scanlon's view fails as an account of how we should treat different-sized groups, non-human animals and cognitively limited human beings. They also argue that Scanlon's contractualism cannot vindicate the common-sense deontic distinctions and that the view must suffer from some form of objectionable circularity or redundancy.

After this, Section 4 introduced how our understanding of consequentialism has changed recently. It explained how consequentialism is today seen as a flexible structural framework in which different versions of consequentialism can be formulated. Section 5 then suggested that we should also understand contractualism in this new way. Most importantly, we should draw a distinction between the general contractualist structural framework and different versions of contractualism that can be generated by formulating the key elements of the contractualist framework in different ways. This framework then enabled us to understand Scanlon's, Parfit's, Southwood's and Gauthier's moral theories as different versions of contractualism that share the same structure. I also argued that the contractualist framework is so flexible that, for any plausible ethical view, there will be a version of contractualism that is co-extensive with it. Finally, Section 5.1 outlined how the previous debates concerning the key objections to Scanlon's contractualism can now be understood as internal disagreements over which version of contractualism is the most plausible one.

This final section concludes by briefly considering what implications this new way of understanding both consequentialism and contractualism has for ethical theorising. It should first be noted that these two general frameworks are not the only ones in which different ethical views can be formulated. There are also many different versions of virtue ethics, Kantian ethics, Rossian pluralism and so on. Perhaps it can be shown that, for any plausible first-order ethical view, there are also versions of these other ethical theories that are co-extensive with it. I will leave it to the defenders of these frameworks to explore this possibility.

Which one of the ethical theories should we then accept if we understand different ethical theories as flexible frameworks in which different ethical views can be represented? Here, I want to suggest that answering this question can no longer be based on which of the ethical theories is 'true' or 'correct'. Let us assume that there is a set of correct verdicts of which actions are right or wrong in every possible situation. If consequentialism and contractualism (and potentially other theories) are as flexible as suggested in this Element, then we know that there are versions of these theories that are correct because they are extensionally equivalent to the previous set of verdicts. After all, these versions of consequentialism and contractualism are right in every situation about the rightness or wrongness of different actions. In this situation, it cannot be the case that the relevant version of consequentialism is more true or correct than the corresponding version of contractualism or vice versa.

Do we then have any other grounds for choosing between the views? Here, I recommend that we should adopt an attitude of *pragmatic pluralism*. We can start from the idea that we can divide our moral beliefs about individual cases into roughly two categories. We have some views about what should be done in different cases that we are very certain about – carefully considered ethical convictions about cases that we could hardly see ourselves giving up. If con sequentialism and contractualism are flexible frameworks, it turns out that there will be versions of these theories that will match the previous convictions. In the case of consequentialism, finding out what the relevant versions of consequentialism are like will often require being inventive in one's theory of value, whereas in the case of contractualism we will often have to develop new theories of reasons. It is true, however, that the resulting versions of consequentialism and contractualism will not tell us anything new – perhaps they can merely help us to represent our prior moral views in clearer, more systematic and more illuminating ways.

In contrast, consider the moral beliefs that we are not very certain about. There are many difficult ethical questions for which we do not confidently know the correct answers, that is, cases in which we do not know which actions are right or wrong. It is here that the different ethical theories understood as flexible frameworks can earn their keep. The flexibility of consequentialism and contractualism enables us to formulate different versions of the views that correspond to different possible solutions to the difficult ethical problems we face. Yet the thing to emphasise about these versions is that they direct our attention to very different kinds of considerations. If we compare the plausibility of different versions of consequentialism as answers to a certain ethical problem, we have to consider different views of which outcomes are good in the given context and why. In contrast, if we compare the plausibility of different versions of contractualism as answers to the same problem, we have to evaluate different views of the reasons that different individuals have for making objections to different principles.

I want to suggest, then, that perhaps *in some cases* considering the different views of what is valuable is a better way to solve the relevant ethical problems. Yet, in other contexts, it might be more useful to consider different accounts of what counts as a good reason to reject a moral principle. Perhaps there are even cases where it is best to do both at the same time. Let me give just two examples. In the climate change ethics for example, it is natural to compare different versions of consequentialism that require very different kinds of climate change actions from us. Versions of consequentialism that discount at a higher rate the harms and benefits which our present actions will cause to future generations will require fewer actions from us than the versions that rely on lower discount rates. Yet comparing the resulting versions of consequentialism seems to be a fruitful way of considering many of the problems of climate change ethics. After all, it is hard to see how we could take into account in any other framework the same amount of information about different climate change scenarios and their probabilities and the vast amount of different potential harms and benefits that different policies will produce for billions of individuals.[42]

However, even if the consequentialist framework were the most useful one for considering the problems of climate change ethics, it would not need to be the most useful framework for pursuing all other difficult ethical questions. Perhaps, for example, when we consider just which promises we are required to keep, it is more fruitful to compare different versions of contractualism formulated in terms of different views of what reasons there are to reject different principles governing promise-keeping. After all, in the relevant promising cases, relatively few individuals are involved and so we can focus on what kinds of standpoints different ethical principles would create for them. Here, perhaps the way forward is to consider which theory of what reasons individuals have for rejecting principles is the most plausible one.

My suggestion, then, is that there is no meaningful general question of which ethical theory is true or correct overall. There probably is a version of every ethical theory that is correct (and, of course, likewise many versions of each theory that are false). Rather, when evaluating the traditional ethical theories understood as flexible frameworks, we should focus on how useful the tools they provide are for solving different difficult moral problems. This is the question of whether, in a case of a given difficult moral problem, it is better to focus on theories of value, reasons, virtue or perhaps consistent, rational willing; and, in advance, we should not rule out the possibility that in different contexts different general ethical frameworks might turn out to provide the best way forward.

This is, of course, not to say that anything goes. Firstly, the different versions of a given ethical theory that are compared in a given domain have to be internally consistent. Secondly, comparing the versions of a given theory

---

[42] This is why much of the work carried out, for example, by the Intergovernmental Panel on Climate Change assumes a framework of expected value consequentialism. For a sketch of how contractualists could try to tackle climate change ethics, see Suikkanen (2014c).

in the context of an ethical problem has to be a fruitful way of approaching that problem – ethical theories will have to earn their keep in this way. Finally, when we have investigated different problems through the lenses of different views, the end results too will need to be a consistent set of verdicts of different cases.

References

Ashford, E. (2003). The demandingness of Scanlon's contractualism. *Ethics*, **113**(2), 273–302.

Bentham, J. (1789/1996). *Introduction to the Principles of Morals and Legislation*, ed. by J. H. Burns and H. L. A. Hart. Oxford: Oxford University Press.

Blackburn, S. (1999). Am I right? *New York Times*, 21 February.

Brand-Ballard, J. (2004). Contractualism and deontic restrictions. *Ethics*, **114**(2), 269–300.

Bratman, M. (1987). *Intention, Plans, and Practical Reason*. Cambridge, MA: Harvard University Press.

Brown, C. (2011). Consequentialize this. *Ethics*, **121**(4), 749–71.

Carlyle, T. (1850/1885). Jesuitism. In T. Carlyle, *Latter-Day Pamphlets*. New York: John B. Alden, pp. 272–313.

Chang, R. (1997). Introduction. In R. Chang, ed., *Incommensurability, Incomparability, and Practical Reason*. Cambridge, MA: Harvard University Press, pp. 1–34.

Dancy, J. (2004). *Ethics without Principles*. Oxford: Oxford University Press.

Doggett, T. (2009). What is wrong with Kamm and Scanlon's arguments against Taurek. *Journal of Ethics and Social Philosophy*, **3**(3), 1–15.

Dreier, J. (1993). Structures of normative theories. *The Monist*, **76**(1), 22–40.

Dreier, J. (2011). In defence of consequentializing. *Oxford Studies in Normative Ethics*, **1**, 97–119.

Foot, P. (1994). Rationality and virtue. In H. Pauer-Studer, ed., *Norms, Values and Society*. Dordrecht: Kluwer, pp. 205–16.

Frick, J. (2015). Contractualism and social risk. *Philosophy and Public Affairs*, **43**(3), 175–223.

Fried, B. (2012). Can contractualism save us from aggregation? *Journal of Ethics*, **16**(1), 39–66.

Gauthier, D. (1986). *Morals by Agreement*. Oxford: Oxford University Press.

Harsanyi, J. (1975). Can the maximin principle serve as a basis for morality? A critique of John Rawls's theory. *The American Political Science Review*, **69**(2), 594–606.

Hieronymi, P. (2011). Of metaethics and motivation: the appeal of contractualism. In R. J. Wallace, R. Kumar and R. Freeman, eds., *Reasons and Recognition – Essays on the Philosophy of T.M. Scanlon*. Oxford: Oxford University Press, pp. 101–28.

Hills, A. (2010). Utilitarianism, contractualism and demandingness. *The Philosophical Quarterly*, **60**(239), 225–242.

Hobbes, T. (1651/1996). *The Leviathan*, ed. by R. Tuck. Cambridge: Cambridge University Press.

Holm, S. (2018). The luckless and the doomed. *Ethical Theory and Moral Practice*, **21**(2), 231–44.

Hooker, B. (2000). *Ideal Code, Real World*. Oxford: Oxford University Press.

Hooker, B. (2003). Contractualism, spare wheel, aggregation. In M. Matravers, ed., *Scanlon and Contractualism*. London: Frank Cass, pp. 53–76.

James, A. (2012). Contractualism's (not so) slippery slope. *Legal Theory*, **18**(3), 263–92.

Kamm, F.M. (2007). *Intricate Ethics: Rights, Responsibilities, and Permissible Harm*. Oxford: Oxford University Press.

Kiesewetter, B. (2017). *The Normativity of Rationality*. Oxford: Oxford University Press.

Kumar, R. (2015). Risking and wronging. *Philosophy and Public Affairs*, **43**(1), 27–43.

Kymlicka, W. (1990). Two theories of justice. *Inquiry*, **33**(1), 99–119.

Lenman, J. (2006). Compatibilism and contractualism: the possibility of moral responsibility. *Ethics*, **117**(1), 7–31.

Locke, J. (1689/2002). *Two Treatises of Government*, ed. by P. Laslett. Cambridge: Cambridge University Press.

Louise, J. (2004). Relative value and the consequentialist umbrella. *Philosophical Quarterly*, **54**(217), 518–36.

McCloskey, H. J. (1965). A non-utilitarian approach to punishment. *Inquiry*, **8**(1–4), 249–263.

McGinn, C. (1999). Reasons and unreasons. *The New Republic*, May 24, 34–8.

Mendus, S. (2003). The magic of the pronoun 'my'. In M. Matravers, ed., *Scanlon and Contractualism*. London: Frank Cass, pp. 33–52.

Mill, J. S. (1861/1998). *Utilitarianism*, ed. by R. Crisp. Oxford: Oxford University Press.

Moehler, M. (2020). *Contractarianism*. Cambridge: Cambridge University Press.

Moore, G. E. (1903). *Principia Ethica*. Cambridge: Cambridge University Press.

Mulgan, T. (2006). *Future People*. Oxford: Oxford University Press.

Norcross, A. (2002). Contractualism and aggregation. *Social Theory and Practice*, **28**(2), 303–14.

Nussbaum, M. (2006). *Frontiers of Justice: Disability, Nationality, Species Membership*. Cambridge, MA: Harvard University Press.

Otsuka, M. (2000). Scanlon and the claims of the many versus the one. *Analysis*, **60**(3), 288–93.

Parfit, D. (1984). *Reasons and Persons*. Oxford: Oxford University Press.

Parfit, D. (2003). Justifiability to each person. *Ratio*, **16**(4), 368–90.

Parfit, D. (2011). *On What Matters*, Vol. 1. Oxford: Oxford University Press.

Pettit, P. (2000). A consequentialist perspective on contractualism. *Theoria*, **66**(3), 228–45.

Phillips, D. (1998). Contractualism and moral status. *Social Theory and Practice*, **24**(2), 183–204.

Plato (*c.* 380 BC/2000). *Republic*, ed. by G. R. F Ferrari, trans. by T. Griffin. Cambridge: Cambridge University Press.

Portmore, D. (2007). Consequentializing moral theories. *Pacific Philosophical Quarterly*, **88**(1), 39–73.

Portmore, D. (2009). Consequentializing. *Philosophy Compass*, **4**(2), 329–47.

Portmore, D. (2011). *Commonsense Consequentialism*. Oxford: Oxford University Press.

Prichard, H. A. (1912). Does moral philosophy rest on a mistake? *Mind*, **21**(81), 21–37.

Rawls, J. (1972). *A Theory of Justice*. Cambridge, MA: Harvard University Press.

Raz, J. (1986). *The Morality of Freedom*. Oxford: Oxford University Press.

Raz, J. (2003). Numbers, with and without aggregation. *Ratio*, **16**(4), 346–67.

Reibetanz, S. (1998). Contractualism and aggregation. *Ethics*, **108**(2), 296–311.

Ridge, M. (2001). Saving Scanlon: contractualism and agent-relativity. *Journal of Political Philosophy*, **9**(4), 472–481.

Ridge, M. (2006). Introducing variable-rate rule-utilitarianism. *Philosophical Quarterly*, **56**(223), 242–256.

Rosen, G. (2009). Might Kantian contractualism be the supreme principle of morality? *Ratio*, **22**(1), 78–97.

Ross, W. D. (1930/2002). *The Right and the Good*, ed. by P. Stratton-Lake. Oxford: Oxford University Press.

Rousseau, J.-J. (1762/1997). *The Social Contract and Other Later Political Writings*, ed. by V. Gourevitch. Cambridge: Cambridge University Press.

Scanlon, T. M. (1982). Contractualism and utilitarianism. In A. Sen and B. Williams, eds., *Utilitarianism and Beyond*. Cambridge: Cambridge University Press, pp. 103–28.

Scanlon, T. M. (1998). *What We Owe to Each Other*. Cambridge, MA: Harvard University Press.

Scanlon, T. M. (2004). Replies. In P. Stratton-Lake, ed., *On What We Owe to Each Other*. Oxford: Blackwell, pp. 123–38.

Scanlon, T. M. (2008). *Moral Dimensions: Permissibility, Meaning, Blame.* Cambridge, MA: Harvard University Press.

Scanlon, T. M. (2013). Reply to Zofia Stemplowska. *Journal of Moral Philosophy,* **10**(4), 508–14.

Scheffler, S. (1982). *The Rejection of Consequentialism.* Oxford: Oxford University Press.

Schroeder, M. (2005). Realism and reduction: the quest for robustness. *Philosophers' Imprint,* **5**(1), 1–18.

Schroeder, M. (2007). Teleology, agent-relative value and 'good'. *Ethics,* **117**(2), 265–95.

Sheinman, H. (2011). Act and principle contractualism. *Utilitas,* **23**(3), 288–315.

Singer, P. (1972). Famine, affluence and morality. *Philosophy and Public Affairs,* **1**(3), 229–243.

Slote, M. (1982). Satisficing consequentialism. *Proceedings of the Aristotelian Society,* suppl. **58**, 139–64.

Smith, H. (2001). Deriving morality from rationality. In P. Vallentyne, ed., *Contractarianism and Rational Choice.* Cambridge: Cambridge University Press, pp. 229–53.

Smith, H. (2010). Measuring the consequences of rules. *Utilitas,* **22**(4), 413–33.

Smith, M. (2003). Neutral and relative value after Moore. *Ethics,* **113**(3), 576–98.

Smith, M. (2009). Two kinds of consequentialism. *Philosophical Issues,* **19**, 257–72.

Southwood, N. (2009). Moral contractualism. *Philosophy Compass,* 4(6), 926–36.

Southwood, N. (2010). *Contractualism and the Foundations of Morality.* Oxford: Oxford University Press.

Southwood, N. (2019). Contractualism for us as we are. *Philosophy and Phenomenological Research,* **99**(3), 529–47.

Stratton-Lake, P. (2003). Scanlon's contractualism and the redundancy objection. *Analysis,* **63**(1), 70–6.

Streumer, B. (2007). Reasons and impossibility. *Philosophical Studies,* **136**(3), 351–84.

Suikkanen, J. (2004). What we owe to many. *Social Theory and Justice,* **30**(4), 485–506.

Suikkanen, J. (2005). Contractualist responses to the redundancy objection. *Theoria,* **71**(1), 38–58.

Suikkanen, J. (2009). Consequentialism, constraints and the good-relative-to: a reply to Mark Schroeder. *Journal of Ethics and Social Philosophy,* **3**(1), 1–8.

Suikkanen, J. (2014a). Consequentialist options. *Utilitas*, **26**(3), 277–301.

Suikkanen, J. (2014b). Contractualism and the conditional fallacy. *Oxford Studies in Normative Ethics*, **4**, 113–37.

Suikkanen, J. (2014c). Contractualism and climate change. In M. Di Paola and G. Pellegrino, eds., *Canned Heat: Ethics and Politics of Climate Change*. London: Routledge, 115–28.

Suikkanen, J. (2017). Contractualism and the counter-culture challenge. *Oxford Studies in Normative Ethics*, **7**, 184–206.

Suikkanen, J. (2019). Ex ante and ex post contractualism: a synthesis. *Journal of Ethics*, **23**(1), 77–98.

Suikkanen, J. (forthcoming). Consequentializing moral dilemmas. *Journal of Moral Philosophy*. https://doi.org/10.1163/17455243-20182787.

Thomson, J. J. (1976). Killing, letting die and the trolley problem. *The Monist*, **59**(2), 204–17.

Thomson, J. J. (1990). *The Realm of Rights*, Cambridge, MA: Harvard University Press.

Timmermann, J. (2004). The individualist lottery: how people count, but not their numbers. *Analysis*, **64**(2), 106–112.

Timmons, M. (2003). The limits of moral constructivism. *Ratio*, **16**(4), 391–423.

Urmson, J. O. (1953). The interpretation of the moral philosophy of J.S. Mill. *The Philosophical Quarterly* **3**(10), 33–9.

Vallentyne, P. (1989). Two types of moral dilemmas. *Erkenntnis*, **30**(3), 301–18.

Vallentyne, P. (2006). Against maximizing act-consequentialism. In J. Dreier, ed., *Contemporary Debates in Moral Theory*. Oxford: Blackwell, pp. 21–37.

Väyrynen, P. (2013). Grounding and normative explanation. *Proceedings of the Aristotelian Society*, suppl. **87**, 155–78.

Wallace, R. J. (2002). Scanlon's contractualism. *Ethics*, **112**(3), 429–70.

Wallace, R. J. (2019). *The Moral Nexus*. Princeton: Princeton University Press.

Cambridge Elements ☰

Elements in Ethics

Ben Eggleston
University of Kansas

Ben Eggleston is a professor of philosophy at the University of Kansas. He is the editor of John Stuart Mill, *Utilitarianism: With Related Remarks from Mill's Other Writings* (Hackett, 2017) and a co-editor of *Moral Theory and Climate Change: Ethical Perspectives on a Warming Planet* (Routledge, 2020), *The Cambridge Companion to Utilitarianism* (Cambridge, 2014), and *John Stuart Mill and the Art of Life* (Oxford, 2011). He is also the author of numerous articles and book chapters on various topics in ethics.

Dale E. Miller
Old Dominion University, Virginia

Dale E. Miller is a professor of philosophy at Old Dominion University. He is the author of *John Stuart Mill: Moral, Social and Political Thought* (Polity, 2010) and a co-editor of *Moral Theory and Climate Change: Ethical Perspectives on a Warming Planet* (Routledge, 2020), *A Companion to Mill* (Blackwell, 2017), *The Cambridge Companion to Utilitarianism* (Cambridge, 2014), *John Stuart Mill and the Art of Life* (Oxford, 2011), and *Morality, Rules, and Consequences: A Critical Reader* (Edinburgh, 2000). He is also the editor-in-chief of *Utilitas*, and the author of numerous articles and book chapters on various topics in ethics broadly construed.

About the Series

This Elements series provides an extensive overview of major figures, theories, and concepts in the field of ethics. Each entry in the series acquaints students with the main aspects of its topic while articulating the author's distinctive viewpoint in a manner that will interest researchers.

Cambridge Elements $\overline{\overline{}}$

Elements in Ethics

Elements in the Series

Printed in the United States
By Bookmasters